The Spiry and Doctrine:

a liturgical-systematic dialogue in the fourth century church in Egypt and Cappadocia

by

Thomas McLean

Contents

1   Introduction   5

2   Egypt: Athanasius and Sarapion   10

3   The Cappadocian Fathers and the
    Anaphoras of St Basil   38

4   Conclusions   63

The cover picture is 'Portrait of a young woman with a gilded wreath', 3rd-4th Century Egypt, currently in the Metropolitan Museum of Art, New York.
This photograph is in the public domain.

List of Abbreviations and Primary Sources

c.	circa
d.	died
ep.	Letter(s)
ET	English Translation
l(l).	line(s)
LXX	The Septuagint
ms(s)	manuscript(s)
or.	Oration/Homily
p(p).	page(s)
tr	translator

Published Series and Editions

ANF   Schaff, Philip (ed), *Ante Nicene Fathers* (T&T Clark, Edinburgh,1996) 10 vols.

DBL   Whitaker, E.C., and Maxwell E. Johnson (eds), *Documents of the Baptismal Liturgy* (3rd edn, SPCK, London, 2003)

FC   *The Fathers of the Church: A New Translation* (Catholic University of America Press, Washington, DC, 1947-) 131+ vols.

GCS   *Die Griechischen christlichen Schriftsteller der ersten drei Jahrhunderte* (Leipzig, 1897-) 53+ vols.

LEW   Brightman, F.E., *Liturgies Eastern and Western, Volume 1 – Eastern* (Clarendon Press, Oxford, 1896)

NPNF   Schaff, Philip (ed), *Nicene and Post-Nicene Fathers* (T&T Clark, Edinburgh, 1996) Series 1 – 14 vols, Series 2 – 14 vols.

PE   Hanggi, Anton, and Irmgard Pahl (eds), *Prex Eucharistica* (Editions Universitaires Fribourge Suisse, Switzerland, 1968)

PEER   Jasper, R. C. D., and G. J. Cuming, *Prayers of the Eucharist: Early and Reformed* (Liturgical Press, Collegeville, Minn.,1990)

PG   Migne, J.P.(ed), *Patrologia Cursus Completus: Series Graeca* (Imprimerie Catholique, Paris,1857) 161 vols.

PL   Migne, J. P.(ed), *Patrologia Cursus Completus: Series Latinae* (Imprimerie Catholique, Paris,1845) 221 vols.

SC   *Sources Chrétiennes* (Les Éditions du Cerf, Paris,1942-) 500+ vols.

Swainson   Swainson, C.A., *The Greek Liturgies* (Cambridge University Press, Cambridge, 1884)

Liturgical Material

A&M	The Anaphora of Addai and Mari
AC	Apostolic Constitutions
BAS	The Anaphora of St. Basil
ArmBAS	The Armenian Recension of BAS
ByzBAS	The Byzantine Recension of BAS, quoted in Greek from PE and in English from PEER.
E-BAS	The Egyptian Recension of BAS

SyrBAS	The Syriac Recension of BAS
CHR	The Anaphora of St. John Chrysostom
GREG	The Anaphora of St. Gregory
JAS	The Anaphora of St. James
MK	The Anaphora of St. Mark

Sarapion The Sacramentary of Sarapion, quoted in Greek and English from Johnson, Maxwell E., *The Prayers of Sarapion of Thmuis: A Literary, Liturgical, and Theological Analysis* (Pontifico Istituto Orientale, Roma, 1995) Orientalia Christiana Analecta 249.

Other anaphoras are given by the name of the traditionally ascribed author. These abbreviations may also refer to the whole liturgy; the distinction should be made by context.

The Works of Athanasius

This list notes only those works cited by abbreviation, and is not a complete bibliography.

De Inc *De Incarnatione*, quoted in Greek and English from John Beir (ed), *On the Incarnation* (St Vladimir's Seminary Press, Yonkers, N.Y, 2011) Popular Patristics Series no. 44a.

OCA *Orationes Contra Arianos*, quoted in English from John Henry Newman (ed), *Select Treatises of S. Athanasius, Archbishop of Alexandria, In Controversy with the Arians* (John Henry Parker, Oxford,1842-4) 2 vols, and quoted in Greek from PG26.

CG *Contra Gentes*, see NPNF2-04.

De Dec *De Decretis*, quoted in English from NPNF2-04, and in Greek from PG25.

De Syn *De Synodis*, see NPNF2-04.

Ad Sarap *Epistulae IV ad Sarapione*, quoted in English from *Works on the Spirit: Athanasius's Letters to Serapion on the Holy Spirit, And, Didymus's On the Holy Spirit* translated by Mark DelCogliano, Andrew Radde-Gallwitz, and Lewis Ayres (St Vladimir's Seminary Press, Yonkers, N.Y, 2011). Popular Patristics Series no. 43.* Quoted in Greek from PG26. Also given as *Letters*.

*Note: The spelling 'Serapion' is used by Brightman and others for 'Sarapion'. Citations here retain the original spelling.

The Works of Basil

This list notes only those works cited by abbreviation, and is not a complete bibliography.

DSS *De Spiritu Sancto*, quoted in Greek from SC17, and in English from Basil, *On the Holy Spirit* translated by Stephen M. Hildebrand (St Vladimir's Seminary Press, Yonkers, N.Y., 2011) Popular Patristics Series no. 42.

Adv Eun *Contra Eunomium*, see FC122.

1

Introduction

In this study, I will explore the extent to which the historical evidence supports a relationship between early pneumatology and liturgical prayer, by comparing the evidence of the *Sacramentary of Sarapion* with the systematic work of Athanasius, and the anaphoras attributed to Basil the Great and the systematic works – for which the attribution is more secure, particularly *De Spiritu Sancto*.

Selection and Methodology

Because of significant lacunae in the record, it is not possible to produce a full history of the relationship between pneumatology and liturgical invocations of the Spirit. With this in mind, these two instances serve as studies of moments in that relationship.

The second half of the fourth century is a time of great development, with Athanasius, bishop of Alexandria, and Basil, bishop of Caesarea, central figures.[1] Both wrote significant treatises on the Holy Spirit, providing a clear insight into their doctrinal approaches. Furthermore, in both cases, there are apparent liturgical connections. In the case of Basil, he is traditionally associated with the liturgy that bears his name. In the case of Athanasius, we do not have his liturgy, but his treatise on the Holy Spirit is addressed to Sarapion of Thmuis. As I shall argue, the so-called *Sacramentary* that bears his name can be justifiably attributed to Sarapion, or at the very least to the correct period and region. Based on their significant influence on the development of the doctrinal

---

[1] For biographies, see Khaled Anatolios, *Athanasius* (Routledge, New York, 2004), 1–39; and Philip Rousseau, *Basil of Caesarea* (University of California Press, Berkeley, 1994) respectively.

Table 1: Syntactical Structures of the Epiclesis[2]

Structure	Features	Examples
1 — Imperative + Imperative (a) 1st verb 'send' (b) 1st verb 'come'	The Father subject of both verbs Spirit, or, occasionally, Son, subject of both verbs	**CHR**, *Severus, Timothy, Philosenus II,* some mss of **MK** *Acts of Thomas*
2 — Imperative + Subordinate (3rd person) clause	Verb always 'send' with Father as subject, 2nd verb has Spirit as subject	**JAS, MK** (2nd epiclesis), **GREG**; all Syriac anaphoras introduced by 'send' in the imperative.
3 — 2nd person singular subjunctive,[3] dependent on an initial verb of supplication + 2nd verb (a) 2nd verb: 3rd sing. Subjunctive (b) 2nd verb: 2nd sing. Subjunctive (c) 2nd verb: imperative	1st verb 'send' addressed to the Father; 2nd verb has the Spirit as the subject The Father subject of both verbs The Father subject of both verbs	**AC**, *Dioynsius the Areopagite* *XII Apostles* An archaic Syrian Orthodox baptismal prayer attributed to Severus
4 — Infinitive + 2nd verb (a) 2nd verb: infinitive (b) 2nd verb: imperative	1st verb is 'come', the Spirit is subject of both 1st verb is 'send', the Father is subject of both	**BAS** Dar Balyzeh Papyrus
5 — All verbs jussive, the Spirit is the subject throughout (a) 1st verb is 'let there (b) reduplication: 'let there be sent and let there come'		Common in East and West Syria Ethiopic usage

---

2 Summarizing Brock, 'Invocations', 382–86.
3 The Syriac examples of this form use the imperfect.

settlement that took form at the Council of Constantinople in 381, and the availability of liturgical material for comparison, these two figures are clear starting points for consideration.

The Epiclesis and its Significance

A brief overview of the development of the epiclesis is necessary to recognize the context of the texts considered here. Brock noted 'The eucharistic epiclesis proves, on close examination, to be a very complex organism whose syntactical structure can vary a great deal', and he thoroughly surveyed the development of the structure, language, and intention in both the Syriac tradition, and the principal Greek texts.[4] Starting from the primitive forms found in 1 Cor. 16.22, Rev. 22.20 and *Didache* 10.6, in the Aramaic phrase transcribed into Greek as μαραναθά,[5] Brock identifies five basic forms, as outlined in Table 1.

In Egypt, a distinctive feature of the Alexandrian tradition is the close association between the Sanctus (without the Benedictus) and the first epiclesis, as well as a second epiclesis after the anamnesis. This tradition is typified by **MK**, in which the first epiclesis is a simple request to the Father for the Holy Spirit to 'fill... this sacrifice' as the heavens are full of God's glory. The second epiclesis provides a distinctive account of the role of the Holy Spirit in salvation history, before the invocation for the Father to send the Spirit 'to sanctify and perfect them', with a long list of fruits of communion.[6]

Until quite recently, much scholarship focused on the anaphora in the so-called *Apostolic Tradition* §4 even if sometimes only to discount its

---

[4] Sebastian P. Brock, 'Invocations To/For the Holy Spirit in Syriac Liturgical Texts: Some Comparative Approaches' in Robert F. Taft and Gabriele Winkler (eds), *Comparative Liturgy Fifty Years after Anton Baumstark (1872-1948), Rome, 25-29 September 1998* (Pontificio Istituto Orientale, Rome, 2001) Orientalia Christiana Analecta 265, here 382. See also Anne Catherine McGowan, *Eucharistic Epicleses, Ancient and Modern: Speaking of the Spirit in Eucharistic Prayers* (SPCK, London, 2014).

[5] Niederwimmer suggests all three can be read as liturgical formulae, *The Didache: A Commentary*, ed. Harold W. Attridge, (Fortress Press, Minneapolis, 1998) 163

[6] ET: PEER pp. 64–66. On the place of the Sanctus here, see Bryan D. Spinks, *The Sanctus in the Eucharistic Prayer* (Cambridge University Press, Cambridge, 1991) 83–93.

epiclesis as interpolation.[7] McGowan's observation that it had a greater influence in the twentieth century than ever before is not ungrounded.[8] Given recent re-evaluations of its provenance,[9] it has dropped from the limelight, but what has been preserved appears to be a relatively simple epiclesis for the fruits of communion, perhaps in the West Syrian pattern in its nascent form.[10]

Table 1: Syntactical Structures of the Epiclesis *(page 6)*

This brief summary shows that there is a broad diversity and variety in forms and language used in liturgical epicleses. Brock concludes, on comparative grounds, that there is a progression in the invocation verb from 'come' to 'let come' to 'send', though not in distinct steps. Further, it appears that an emphasis on the consecration of the elements tends to be later, and on fruits of communion earlier, though both also can show different strata of development. It is also hard to identify whether there is a single point of origin or a greater diversity that has homogenized.[11] In light of this, more caution is required than expressed by older scholarship on the origins of the epiclesis.

The Doctrinal Context

The two examples considered here stem from the most active stage of the development of the theology of the Holy Spirit. It was the period of the Arian crisis; and the responses to it, from the Council of Nicaea at the beginning of the fourth century through to the Council of Constantinople at the end, saw the greatest creativity in attempting to penetrate the mystery of the nature of the Trinity, and laid the foundations for all that

---

[7] cf. Gregory Dix, 'The Origins of the Epiclesis' in *Theology* 28 (1934) 133.
[8] McGowan, *Eucharistic Epicleses*, 80.
[9] See Paul F. Bradshaw, Maxwell E. Johnson, and L. Edward Philips, *The Apostolic Tradition* (Augsburg Fortress, Minneapolis, 2002).
[10] McGowan, *Eucharistic Epicleses*, 78–80
[11] McGowan, *Eucharistic Epicleses*, 85–86; Sebastian P. Brock, 'Towards a Typology of the Epicleses in the West Syrian Anaphoras' in Hans-Jürgen Feulner, Elena Velkovska, and Robert F. Taft (eds), *Crossroad of Cultures: Studies in Liturgy and Patristics in Honor of Gabriele Winkler* (Pontificio Istituto Orientale, Rome, 2000) Orientalia Christiana Analecta 260, 187–89.

comes after. Prior to this period, there are few developed ideas regarding the person of the Spirit, but by the end of the period treatises on the topic have become possible.

✱✱✱

Noting this diversity of form and style of liturgical invocation of the Holy Spirit in early sources, and the nascent development of understanding of the nature and person of the Holy Spirit within the fourth century church, I will examine these two case studies, of Athanasius and Sarapion in Egypt, and of Basil in Cappadocia, and explore what evidence there is to demonstrate the nature of the relationship between the liturgical texts and the dogmatic positions that develop.

2

Egypt: Athanasius and Sarapion

Athanasius was one of the most significant figures in the development of what became the orthodox position in Trinitarian theology. Compared to many contemporaries, he made far less use of liturgical material in his writings, and there is nothing extant of the liturgy of Alexandria in his day. However, the document known as the *Sacramentary of Sarapion* is ascribed to his friend and correspondent Sarapion, bishop of nearby Thmuis.

This chapter will begin with a consideration of Athanasius' theology of the Holy Spirit. I will consider firstly the Trinitarian thinking underlying his anti-Arian writings, and then look more closely at the pneumatology in his *Letters to Sarapion*. I will then look at the *Sacramentary*, and, through a general overview of the whole document, I will argue as probable that the editor responsible for this collection was indeed the same Sarapion with whom Athanasius corresponded on the Holy Spirit. This is followed by a closer examination of the texts of the two epicleses of the anaphora, the epiclesis of the prayer of blessing of the water for baptism, and the prayer for the ordination of presbyters. I will show that Athanasius' conception of the Holy Spirit may present a way of understanding the pneumatological implications of the λόγος epicleses in the anaphora and the baptism prayer. Furthermore, I shall argue that the first epiclesis of the anaphora could have been understood in a Trinitarian manner. Finally, from the ordination prayer, I will show that there is no doubt that the editor of the collection clearly held that the Holy Spirit was indeed fully divine, and was not part of the pneumatomachian group opposed by Athanasius and Sarapion.

Athanasius and his Anti-Arian Works

While Athanasius was renowned for his Christological contributions in the Arian controversy, his thought was not limited to this. Nevertheless, there is no case directly presented for the Trinity *per se* in his main works. Yet, threaded through them, there is a clear sense of a Trinitarian understanding of God, which begins to be spelt out clearly in **Ad Sarap**, which stands upon the relationship between the Father and the Son spelt out in the earlier works and utilizes a method rooted in the same approach to the exegesis of Scripture.

Unlike many patristic theologians, Athanasius does not make frequent reference to liturgical formulae. Amongst his anti-Arian works, there are limited doxological references, as well as consideration of baptism. **De Inc** concludes with the doxology: 'in Christ Jesus our Lord, through whom and with whom, to the Father with the Son himself in the Holy Spirit [ἐν ἁγίῳ Πνεύματι], be honour and power and glory to the ages of ages.'[12] Similarly, in **De Dec**, we find 'because to God and the Father is due the glory, honour, worship with his co-existing Son and Word, together with the All-holy and Life-giving Spirit [ἅμα τῷ παναγίῳ καὶ ζωοποιῷ Πνεύματι], now and unto endless ages of ages.'[13] For Athanasius, these types of doxology seem to function as a definite statement of the divinity of each of the three persons. These statements describe, in Weinandy's summary, the 'foundation for the distinction between the Father, the Son, and the Holy Spirit as well as their equality as the one God'.[14] It is the act of worship, for Athanasius, that confirms the divinity of each, with a distinct identity. It is however noteworthy that Athanasius displays a reticence over the use of the term ὑπόστασις perhaps fearing it implied tritheism.[15]

The baptismal formula is used by Athanasius in a similar way both

---

[12] **De Inc** 57
[13] **De Dec** VIII.32
[14] Thomas G. Weinandy, *Athanasius: A Theological Introduction, Great Theologians Series* (Ashgate, Aldershot, 2007), 103.
[15] John Behr, The Nicene Faith, *The Formation of Christian Theology*, v. 2 (St. Vladimir's Seminary Press, Crestwood, 2004) 247–49.

in **De Dec**,[16] and in **OCA**, where he writes, 'whom the Father baptizes, him the Son baptizes; and whom the Son baptizes, he is consecrated in the Holy Ghost [οὗτος ἐν Πνεύματι ἁγίῳ τελειοῦται].'[17] Whilst not exploring the person of the Spirit, his logic requires the Spirit's divinity: otherwise, his case for the divinity of the Son fails, for it requires the same foundations. He proceeds to argue that the Arian baptism is flawed because they understand the formula to refer to baptism 'into Creator and creature and into Maker and work' rather than into Father and Son.[18] The same reduction applies if the Spirit is not equally divine.

These limited examples show that, despite having other concerns more pressing for his primary attention – namely the Arians – there is a clear belief in the divinity of the Spirit to be found in Athanasius' early, polemical works. As this shows, even though he is not explicit, his argument against the Arian party depends on this.

The Letters to Sarapion

This implicit Trinitarianism in Athanasius' anti-Arian writings, is made explicit in his later works. In **Ad Sarap**, Athanasius is not writing against Arians, but those whom he calls *Tropikoi*, who appear to be a group with pneumatomachian tendencies. The title *Tropikoi* is unexplained; DelCogliano et al. suggest we may translate it is as 'Mis-interpreters', i.e. as cognate to τροπος: the dispute seems centred around the correct means of interpreting Scripture.[19] It is not obvious that the change is because the Athanasian party has 'won' – Athanasius acknowledges that he is in exile.[20]As portrayed by Athanasius, the group seem to be influenced by the Arian theology of Eunomius and Aetius.[21]

---

[16] **De Dec** VII.30.
[17] **OCA** II.41.
[18] **OCA** II.42
[19] Mark DelCogliano, Andrew Radde-Gallwitz, and Lewis Ayres (eds), *Works on the Spirit: Athanasius's Letters to Serapion on the Holy Spirit, and, Didymus's On the Holy Spirit* (St. Vladimir's Seminary Press, Yonkers, NY, 2011) 21
[20] **Ad Sarap** 1.1.1.
[21] DelCogliano, Radde-Gallwitz, and Ayres, Works on the Spirit, 28; Anatolios, *Athanasius*, 212. Sarapion's side of the correspondence has not survived, nor have works from the group in question.

As in his other works, Athanasius is firm that Scripture does not stand alone, and can only be correctly interpreted with the understanding of its σκοπός: the revelation of God through Jesus Christ. He also deviates from what might be termed the Alexandrian school, in not resorting to allegorism as a dominant tool – though without rejecting it altogether. Kannengiesser's description of Athanasius as 'the inventor of… "dogmatic exegesis"' is apt.[22] The position of the *Tropikoi* seems to be that the Holy Spirit is a mere creature. Athanasius' response is to seek to prove, from Scripture, that the Holy Spirit has a 'relationship of unity' with the Son, analogous to that of the Son with the Father - though he does not wish to establish that the relationships are identical.[23]

In structure, the first letter begins with Athanasius' personal comments to Sarapion (1.1 – 2), before beginning with an exegesis of the passages that seem to be being put forward by his opponents, Amos 4.13 and 1 Timothy 5.21 (1.3-14).[24] Athanasius then moves on to discuss the relationships between the Father, the Son and the Holy Spirit, and the question that seems to have been put as to whether the Spirit is in fact a second Son, or a Grandson (1.15–21). He then offers exegesis of a number of other passages to establish the relationship between the Spirit and the Son (1.22–27), before closing with reference to the Trinity and the unity of the Godhead (1.28–33).

The second letter is written in response to a request for an epitome (see 2.1.1). However, that is not what Athanasius produced. Instead, we have a tract on the divinity of the Son (2.1–9), followed by an abridgement of 1.22–31 (2.10–16), wherein no discussion is given to the themes of the first part of the first letter. The third letter covers similar territory to 1.15-21, though it is not a recapitulation, but a fresh examination.[25]

---

[22] Charles Kannengiesser, 'Athanasius of Alexandria and the Foundation of Traditional Christology' in *Theological Studies* 34, no. 1 (March 1973) 110.

[23] Michael A. G. Haykin, *The Spirit of God: The Exegesis of 1 and 2 Corinthians in the Pneumatomachian Controversy of the Fourth Century*, Supplements to Vigiliae Christianae 27 (Brill, Leiden, 1994) 63–66. I follow the numbering of the edition of DelCogliano, Radde-Gallwitz, and Ayres, *Works on the Spirit*

[24] I follow the numbering of the edition of DelCogliano, Radde-Gallwitz, and Ayres, *Works on the Spirit*

[25] Haykin, *Spirit of God*, 62.

Athanasius' Conception of the Holy Spirit

Athanasius' theology of the Holy Spirit is profoundly rooted in his understanding of the unity, and ineffability of God, and rests upon his absolute distinction between creature and Creator. He argues strongly for the status of the Holy Spirit on the side of the Creator in **Ad Sarap** 1.22.1, where he observes how Scripture, quoting Gen.1.1, counts creatures as made from nothing, ἐξ οὐκ ὄντων, whereas, on the basis of 1 Cor.2.11-12, he describes the Spirit as being from God, ἐκ τοῦ θεοῦ. He proceeds to note 'The one who is from God cannot be from nothing, nor can he be a creature – unless they think that the one from whom the Spirit comes is also a creature!' (1.22.1). The necessary consequence of this, though Athanasius never states it outright, is that the Spirit must be Creator, i.e., party to the creative activity of God.[26] The closest Athanasius gets to this is calling the Spirit 'life-giving', ζωοποιὸν, and that creatures are given life through him (1.23.2-3). Further, he emphasizes that the Spirit does not 'participate [μετέχον] in life, but is himself participated [μετεχόμενον] in and gives life to creatures' (1.23.3).

The Spirit's place in creation is confirmed by the Spirit's work in sanctification. Athanasius draws on descriptions of the Spirit as the Spirit of sanctification, ἁγιωσύνης, and renewal, ἀνακαινώσεώς.[27] This is followed by a reference to Psalm 104, which suggests that for Athanasius creation, κτισθήσονται, is equivalent to renewal.[28]Athanasius' purpose in making this point is to prove that the Spirit is God, as only God can create and sanctify, but creation and sanctification seems to be the particular work of the Spirit.

For Athanasius, if the Spirit is divine, then the Spirit shares in the nature of God. This becomes most apparent in his consideration of the question posed, perhaps in jest, of whether the Spirit should be considered as a second Son or a Grandson.[29] Here, Athanasius could

---

[26] Ibid., 78.
[27] Here at **Ad Sarap** 1.22.3-4, he quotes Rom. 1.4, Titus 3.4-7
[28] **Ad Sarap** 1.22.5. Whilst Migne's edition continues the quotation 'and you renew the face of the earth', DelCogliano *et al.*, following newer critical editions, omit this..
[29] **Ad Sarap** 1.15.

be seen as providing a weak answer to the question, in that he insists the revelation in Scripture should be enough. He refuses to answer the question, and instructs Sarapion not to. Quoting 1 Corinthians 2.10-11, he condemns – in something of an *ad hominem* attack – those who seek to search the unknowable depths of God. Using the same text, he also argues for the divinity of the Spirit, for knowing the 'depths of God' means the Spirit must share in that nature.

Another characteristic of God that Athanasius argues transfers to the Spirit is that of uniqueness. Here Athanasius appears to apply, as an epistemological principle, that knowledge of God begins in Jesus Christ. Thus, knowledge of God only comes through the Spirit of Christ, that is, the Holy Spirit. As the Spirit cannot thus be separated from the Son, the Spirit must share in the nature of the Son, except in that of being the Son. That therefore includes his uniqueness. This oneness seems also to extend back: if the Spirit were not unique that would add complexity to the Godhead, rendering the Trinity not one, and instead would leave the Spirit in the same position as the creatures.[30]

This relationship between the Son and the Spirit is central for Athanasius. It is typical of his method to describe the relationship of the Spirit to the Son as analogous to that between the Son and the Father.[31]He focuses on this to a sufficient extent that, as a modern critic, Sergius Bulgakov can accuse Athanasius of providing two dyads, Father-Son and Son-Spirit, rather than a true Trinitarian theology.[32]This relation is shown in the development of metaphorical imagery of the Father as a fountain, the Son as the river, and the Holy Spirit as a draught. Yet when Athanasius clarifies this he writes 'when we drink of the Spirit, we drink of Christ' – he does not link the Spirit directly to the Father.[33] Likewise, when asking the consequences of the Spirit being a creature, it

---

[30] **Ad Sarap** 1.27, 2.12.5-13.3, OCA III.15. cf. Haykin, *Spirit of God*, 83–86..
[31] Ibid., 66.
[32] It should be observed that Bulgakov does not find anything he considers a satisfactory Trinitarianism anywhere in the Patristic era. See *The Comforter* (William B. Eerdmans, Grand Rapids, 2004) 26
[33] **Ad Sarap** 1.19.4..

is primarily the implication to the Son that he draws out – namely, that the Son also would have to be a creature.[34] This link is again presented when Athanasius considers the Spirit as unction (χρίσμα), where the Spirit is associated with the Son as his 'fragrance', and it is through this unction that the Son then joins the anointed to the Father.[35]

This is another characteristic of the Spirit that is drawn out strongly by Athanasius. It is through the Spirit that we can participate in God, which for Athanasius is tantamount to the question of salvation. He writes that 'the seal [the Spirit] has the form of Christ… those who are sealed participate in him'.[36] Elsewhere, 'If the Holy Spirit were a creature, we would not have participation in God through him.'[37] This is not limited to **Ad Sarap**; in his anti-Arian writings, he writes, 'by the participation of the Spirit we are knit into the Godhead'.[38] Athanasius' use of the imagery of the 'temple of God' serves to illustrate the same point, based on Paul's connection that those who are the temple of God have the Spirit of God dwelling in them.[39]

The Sacramentary of Sarapion

The document referred to as the *Sacramentary of Sarapion* is taken from a single eleventh century manuscript found in the library of the Monastery of the Great Lavra on Mt. Athos. The manuscript consists of 186 leaves, though only fourteen contain the Sacramentary, the remainder containing portions of the Septuagint. It was first published in 1894. The first English edition was that of F.E. Brightman in 1900, with only a limited number of further translations, the most recent of which is that of Maxwell Johnson.[40]

The document contains thirty prayers, each individually titled. Since

---

[34] **Ad Sarap** 1.21.1..
[35] **Ad Sarap** 2.12.1-3..
[36] **Ad Sarap** 1.23.7.'
[37] **Ad Sarap** 1.24.2..
[38] **OCA** III.24.
[39] 1 Cor 3.16; **Ad Sarap** 2.12.14-15.
[40] Maxwell E. Johnson, *The Prayers of Sarapion of Thmuis: A Literary, Liturgical, and Theological Analysis* (Pontifico Istituto Orientale, Rome, 1995) Orientalia Christiana Analecta 249, 23–24.

first publication the correct ordering of these prayers has been disputed. Following Johnson, I refer to the prayers by number, according to the order they occur in the manuscript. Brightman argued that the prayers are in no particular order, and in his work offered a re-ordering to construct a rudimentary sacramentary.[41] This order has been adopted in a number of editions, amongst them that of R.J.S. Barrett-Lennard.[42] Geoffrey Cuming also proposes a reordering, placing prayers 15-30, with the title 'Προσευχ Σαραπίωνος Θμούεως' that occurs before 15 at the heading of the text, followed by prayers 1-14.[43] Johnson presents a good case that the prayers themselves are sufficiently an anthology, rather than the composition of a single hand, and that it seems over-ambitious to attempt a reordering as Brightman does.[44] However, if a reordering must be done, Cuming's proposal is supported by the rubric that occurs after Prayer 30, 'All these prayers are accomplished before the prayer of offering', and can be explained as a simple error by a copyist beginning on the wrong side of the manuscript being duplicated, realizing the error, and adding a note of explanation.[45]

Before analyzing the contents of the prayers themselves, it is necessary to consider briefly some of the arguments involved in trying to place this text in its *Sitz im Leben*. The titles within the text before the first prayer in the manuscript, the anaphora, and before prayer 15 include the name Sarapion, but given the propensity of pseudonymity in texts of this type from this period, we cannot presume authorial identity.[46]

Bernard Botte argued that these texts are definitely not by Sarapion,

---

[41] F. E. Brightman, 'The Sacramentary of Serapion of Thmuis' in *The Journal of Theological Studies* os-I, no. 1 (1899): 88–113, https://doi.org/10.1093/jts/os-I.1.88; F. E. Brightman, 'The Sacramentary of Serapion of Thmuis' in *The Journal of Theological Studies* os-I, no. 2 (1900): 247–77, https://doi.org/10.1093/jts/os-I.2.247.

[42] R. J. S. Barrett-Lennard, *The Sacramentary of Sarapion of Thmuis: A Text for Students* (Alcuin/ GROW *Joint Liturgical Study* 25 Grove Books, Bramcote, Nottingham, 1993).

[43] R. J. S. Barrett-Lennard, *The Sacramentary of Sarapion of Thmuis: A Text for Students* (Alcuin/ GROW *Joint Liturgical Study* 25 Grove Books, Bramcote, Nottingham, 1993).

[44] Johnson, *Prayers of Sarapion*, 279–80.

[45] Cuming, 'Thmuis', 569–70.

[46] cf. Geoffrey J. Cuming, 'Pseudonymity and Authenticity, with Special Reference to the Liturgy of St John Chrysostom' in *Studia Patristica* 15 (Akademie, Berlin, 1984) 532–38..

but instead are the work of a later writer with Arian or Pneumatomachian inclinations.[47] Whilst we shall more thoroughly consider the most significant prayers in this regard shortly, it is worthwhile to consider briefly Botte's case here. Botte argues that the Father is largely considered only as ἀγένητος (uncreated), as distinct from ἀγέννητος (unbegotten), with the potential implication of considering the Son to thus be γενητός (created). Going further, Botte suggests there is no statement of the Son's divinity. He additionally suggests that a deliberate attempt is made to subordinate the Spirit, through limited use of a definite article, the absence of the Spirit from the blessing of the oils (prayers 15-17) and being replaced in the epicleses of both the blessing of the water (prayer 7) and the anaphora (1) with an invocation of the λόγος.[48]

As Johnson notes, if a redactor was trying to reduce the role of the Holy Spirit, we must question why the redactor has four references to the Spirit in the Preface, which are largely without parallel elsewhere. Furthermore, the case over the use of the term ἀγένητος is weak: Sarapion mostly uses the term in connection with the title 'Father', and only addresses ἀγένητος θεός in passages directly addressed to the Father.[49] On this point, Catherine Mowry LaCugna writes,[50]

> The God addressed in prayer is now often named 'Father of the Only-Begotten Son'. The substitution of 'Son' for 'Christ' highlights the divinity of Christ... With the insertion of the Holy Spirit into the doxology as mediator alongside Christ, and the increasingly common reference to Christ as the only-begotten, the name of God as Father takes on a more pronounced intratrinitarian meaning. This is in

---

[47] Bernard Botte, 'L'Eucologe de Sérapion Est-Il Authentique' in *Oriens Christianus* 48 (1964) 52, 54–55 especially.

[48] Mazza takes Botte's conclusions, and also suggests that the redactor was an archaizer. I suggest that this is not worthy of separate consideration once Botte's is shown to have no merit, as the later date Botte assumes may require an archaizer that is unnecessary with an earlier date. See Enrico Mazza, *The Origins of the Eucharistic Prayer* (Liturgical Press, Collegeville, 1995) 219–239 (221).

[49] Johnson, *Prayers of Sarapion*, 238–39.

[50] Catherine Mowry LaCugna, *God for Us: The Trinity and Christian Life* (Harper San Francisco, New York, 2006) 115–16.

keeping with concurrent doctrinal developments. As we have seen, prior to the fourth century, in the Bible and early creeds and in Greek theology, Father was a synonym for God and did not denote God's special eternal relationship as Begetter of the Son.

This development locates the description of the Father as ἀγένητος, as a firmly anti-Arian description. Alongside this we can sit Athanasius himself, who counts the term as not to be preferred, but as acceptable.[51] As we shall see in the next chapter, Basil, writing at the end of the fourth century, while arguing for a coordinate doxology, can find no reason to reject the uncoordinate form.[52] From the anointing prayers, it seems that Sarapion preserves an earlier pattern without a post-baptismal anointing, and thus we should be cautious over where we would expect the Spirit to appear.[53] This leaves only the epicleses in Botte's case, to which I shall return later.

Whilst Botte has attempted to put the case that these prayers do not belong in the milieu of fourth century Egypt, Johnson – following Cuming – has attempted to restate that hypothesis. Johnson does note the difficulty in having confidence of the involvement of Sarapion himself in the assembly of the collection. We do not have a substantial collection of his writings, and what we do have does not provide convenient parallels for comparison.[54] Even if we did, assuming this collection is an anthology, it would not be surprising to find only matches which we could not distinguish from the *Formelgut* out of which any liturgical text of the corresponding period and context would be formed. Yet why

---

[51] See **De Dec** 7,30-31; **De Syn** III:47
[52] See, for example, his **DSS** 25,59.
[53] On the questions of the pattern of initiation in the fourth century in Alexandria, see Paul F. Bradshaw, 'Baptismal Practice in the Alexandrian Tradition, Eastern or Western?' in Paul F. Bradshaw (ed), *Essays in Early Eastern Initiation* (Alcuin/GROW Joint Liturgical Study 8, Grove Books, Bramcote, Nottingham, 1988). However, note the questions raised by Bryan D. Spinks, 'Sarapion of Thmuis and Baptismal Practice in Early Christian Egypt: The Need for a Judicious Reassessment' in *Worship* 72, no. 3 (May 1998) 255–70.
[54] cf. Johnson, *Prayers of Sarapion*, 282–84. The main authentic works of Sarapion extant are a letter *Against the Manichees* and *Ad monachos*.

would it be attributed falsely to Sarapion? A more illustrious candidate, such as Athanasius himself, would serve better than a bishop of a minor diocese of the Nile Delta. At the very least, it seems appropriate to accept, in the words of Brightman, 'the name of Serapion can at least stand as a symbol of the date and provenance of the prayers'[55]

The thirty prayers of the collection itself present material for a variety of liturgical situations. Most have very limited relevance to our discussion here. Almost all the texts finish with a Trinitarian doxology, in a coordinated form. Perhaps in Egypt, where the influence of Origen remained strong, and given his assertion that prayer should be directed only to God the Father through Christ, this should be unsurprising.[56] Nevertheless, as we noted above, in the Athanasian mind-set, placing the Holy Spirit alongside the Father and the Son in this way states the Spirit's divinity.

I will, however, give greater attention to a number of items. Firstly, within the anaphora there are two epicleses. The latter of these is most famous, as a unique example of a eucharistic epiclesis of the λόγος. We will also consider the invocation over the water in prayer 7, which as previously noted also invokes the λόγος, and the prayer for the ordination of presbyters (13), which in contrast to the other key texts here, is very explicit in its reference to the Spirit.

The Δύναμις epiclesis

Beside you stand the two most-honoured six-winged seraphim. With two wings they cover the face, and with two the feet, and with two they fly; sanctifying. With them receive also our sanctification as we say: Holy, holy, holy Lord of Sabaoth; heaven and earth are full of your glory. Full is heaven and full also is the earth of your

---

[55] Brightman, 'Sacramentary (Pt.1)' 91.

[56] cf. *Contra Celsum* 5.4. Note, however, that the position of Origen was actually more complex than this – see Paul F. Bradshaw, 'God, Christ and the Holy Spirit in Early Christian Praying' in Bryan D.Spinks (ed), *The Place of Christ in Liturgical Prayer: Trinity, Christology, and Liturgical Theology* (Liturgical Press, Collegeville, 2008) 57–58.

majestic glory, Lord of powers. Fill also this sacrifice with your power and with your participation. For to you we offered this living sacrifice, the unbloody offering.

σοὶ παραστήκουσιν τὰ δύο τιμιώτατα σεραφεὶμ ἐξαπτέρυγα, δυσίν μὲν πτέρυξιν καλύπτοντα τὸ πρόσωπον, δυσὶ δὲ τοὺς πόδας, δυσὶ δὲ πετόμενα, καὶ ἁγιάζοντα· μεθ᾽ ὧν δέξαι καὶ τὸν ἡμέτερον ἁγιασμὸν λεγόντων Ἅγιος ἅγιος ἅγιος κύριος σαβαὼθ πλήρης ὁ οὐρανὸς καὶ ἡ γῆ τῆς δόξης σου. Πλήρης ἐστιν ὁ οὐρανός, πλήρης ἐστὶν καὶ ἡ γῆ τῆς μεγαλοπρεποῦς σου δόξης κύριε τῶν δυνάμεων· πλήρωσον καὶ τὴν θυσίαν ταύτην τῆς σῆς δυνάμεως καὶ τῆς σῆς μεταλήψεως· σοὶ γὰρ προσηνέγκαμεν ταύτην τὴν ζῶσαν θυσίαν τὴν προσφορὰν τὴν ἀναίμακτον.

The first epiclesis of the anaphora in the Sacramentary exhibits one of the features of the anaphora that seems to be distinctive to the Egyptian tradition: the close association of the invocation to the Sanctus, which, unlike in the Syrian tradition, does not feature the Benedictus. Given the similarities of the Preface to the equivalent passage in **MK** – indeed preserving what seems to be the earlier readings found in Coptic manuscripts, rather than material imported from **JAS** as the Greek version does – it seems reasonable to conclude that this preserves something of an earlier version of **MK**.[57] We will explore here the implications of this structure for the meaning of the epiclesis that follows.

Power

Mary K. Farag, in her consideration of this epiclesis, notes the use of δύναμις by Athanasius as a title for the Son.[58] She suggests that for Athanasius, Christ is uniquely the Power of God, and that as such the

---

[57] Johnson, *Prayers of Sarapion*, 205–8. This may strictly be common ancestry, rather than giving precedence to **MK**, nonetheless the result is the same.
[58] Note also that there is wider debate regarding the Son as δύναμις in Egypt; see Mark Edwards' comments on Clement of Alexandria, *Catholicity and Heresy in the Early Church* (Ashgate, Farnham, 2009) 65–66.

title is second only to 'Word' as a title for the second person of the Trinity (presumably distinct from 'Son' as his proper name). This status is, Farag notes, demonstrated by the works which Christ performs, most notably that 'the Son effects his own resurrection by virtue of being Power'.[59] Farag, turning her attention to the Athanasian approach to the Spirit, notes how the Spirit is never simply 'Power' but always the 'Spirit of Power'. The distinction, she suggests, is most visible in his consideration of the annunciation,[60] where Athanasius seems to draw a distinction between 'the Holy Spirit shall come upon you' and 'the Power of the Most High will overshadow you'. Athanasius, though, is very clear over the unity of the action, that 'the Spirit was in the Word'.[61] It seems he wants to identify two features to the annunciation: the coming of the Spirit, and the coming of the Word – that is the Power of the Most High.

This distinction must deal with the question of what Paul describes as works worked by the power of the Spirit. Farag observes that Athanasius sees this expression as referring to the work of the Spirit in creation, rather than in relation to the Father and the Son. This is particularly shown in the way Athanasius unpacks the phrase in relation to Christ. Here, it appears Athanasius is keen to emphasize its relation to Christ's flesh, 'He being said, as man, to have received…'[62] It is, therefore, clear that, in the Athanasian tradition, the term δύναμις can be understood as a title for Christ.

As Farag notes, the δύναμις epiclesis is not unique to the Sacramentary, with surviving examples also being found in initiation liturgies in the *Acts of Thomas* (two instances) and the Coptic Orthodox rites (seven prayers), and one other eucharistic example in the British Museum Tablet.[63] The latter of these, as I shall note below, is very similar to the Sacramentary text, and can clearly be read in the same light as this text.

---

[59] Mary K. Farag, 'Dynamis Epicleses: An Athanasian Perspective' in *Studia Liturgica* 39, no. 1 (1 January 2009) 64-68 (66)
[60] Athanasius' exegesis of Luke 1.35 in **Ad Sarap** 2.15.2.
[61] **Ad Sarap** 2.15.3.
[62] **OCA** I.50. cf. Farag, 'Dynamis Epicleses', 71–72
[63] Ibid., 73–74.

The two texts from the *Acts of Thomas* require interpretation: the text in the account of the baptism of Mygdonia associates power with Christ, but as an attribute; the text from the baptism of Gundaphorus can be read as containing two parallel invocations, the first calling Christ by name, the second by title ('power'). The other use of power in an epiclesis in the Sacramentary is perhaps in the same model as the former of these. The examples from the Coptic Orthodox Baptismal Liturgy do not reflect a univocal position. Farag suggests five of the seven, along with the text from the Sacramentary and the British Museum Tablet support the Athanasian understanding. Only one explicitly connects 'power' with the Holy Spirit, directly as 'the power of thy Holy Spirit', but this then directly incorporates the concept of participation which must stand as the other part of such an Athanasian reading.[64]

Participation

This understanding of the term δύναμις is only able to address one part of this epiclesis. However, it is not just the δύναμις that is invoked here, but also the μετάληψις. Unlike δύναμις, μετάληψις is only used rarely by Athanasius. In these cases, it concerns the participation of the Son in the Father, and as such expresses the divinity of the Son because he participates in the Father.[65] The word is used on two other occasions in the Sacramentary: firstly, in prayer 2, where the implication is regarding the fruits of communion; it is also used in prayer 5, where it appears to be concerned with the blessing of oil and water for healing.

The concept of participation is found in the works of Athanasius, expressed through words such as μετουσιά, μετοχή and their cognates, and has a particular connection to the Holy Spirit. Along with the examples of this usage noted above, Kannengiesser draws particular attention to **OCA** I.46-51. He suggests that here we can see that the 'divine

---

[64] The text is quoted by Farag, Ibid., 74.
[65] There are just two examples, both in **De Syn**, recorded in Guido Muller (ed), *Lexicon Athanasium* (Walter De Gruyter & Co., Berlin, 1952).

pneuma is entirely oriented to the realization of salvation', which as we have noted, for Athanasius, is concerned with participation in the Godhead. It is through our participation in the Spirit that we partake of God.[66]

As indicated, this parallels the form of MK preserved in the British Museum Tablet. There, we have an epiclesis that reads 'send your Holy Spirit and your power on these set before you'.[67] It is possible that this preserves a parallel development to the text of Sarapion, where 'participation' has been spelt out as the Holy Spirit, or at very least indicates such a combination may have existed within the *Formelgut* in Egypt in the fourth century.

While we cannot make as strong a case for the use of 'Participation' for the Spirit as we can for 'Power' as a title for the Son, there is a clear sense in which causing us to participate in the Godhead is the work of the Spirit. We must then consider what the epiclesis connotes in this context.

The Connection of the Sanctus and the Epiclesis

The conjunction of the two seraphim with the 'face' they cover is particularly interesting. It is unusual as, with the exception of the Deir Balyzeh papyrus, the **MK** tradition refers to 'faces', following Isaiah. Origen makes use of the idea in his early imagery for the Trinity, suggesting the seraphim to be the Son and the Spirit covering the face of the Father. Origen writes, 'those two seraphim in Isaiah, which are described as having each six wings, and calling to one another, and saying, "Holy, holy, holy is the Lord God of hosts," were to be understood of the only-begotten Son of God and of the Holy Spirit.[68] While Origen has in mind the biblical text of Isaiah 6.2-3, rather than liturgical usage

---

[66] Charles Kannengiesser, 'Athanasius of Alexandria and the Holy Spirit between Nicea I and Constantinople I' in *Irish Theological Quarterly* 48, no. 3–4 (1981): 174. cf. **OCA** I.50.

[67] ET: PEER p.56. PEER presents a combined version of the John Rylands Papyrus and the British Museum Tablet. The texts are presented separately, albeit in the case of the British Museum Tablet reconstructed into Greek, by Cuming; see Geoffrey J. Cuming, *The Liturgy of St Mark* (Pontificum Institutum Studiorum Orientalium, Rome, 1990) *Orientalia Christiana Analecta* 234, 64–66. Note that the otherwise very similar John Rylands version does not contain the invocation of 'power'.

[68] *De Principiis* I.3.4. SC 252 p. 148. ET: ANF04 p.253. Origen does ascribe this to his Hebrew teacher. See also IV.1.24.

– in a parallel passage, he cites the Sanctus in that form rather than the liturgical form – it is possible that this form of imagery influences the form of the epiclesis that occurs here.[69]

It is by no means certain this has influenced Sarapion. Spinks has suggested that Origen is not the primary influence, and we should connect the two seraphim with the living creatures of Habakkuk 3.2 LXX.[70] Spinks suggests the interpretation 'Christ and the Holy Spirit speak in us, so that we, like the living creatures who stand beside you, may praise you with the Holy, holy, holy.'[71] This line of argument stems from the expression in the Preface 'Let the Lord Jesus speak in us and let holy Spirit also hymn you through us' and thus the focus should be on their indwelling in the worshipper.

Johnson suggests that Spinks misplaces the emphasis. While Spinks focuses on 'us' and 'we', Johnson argues we should place the focus on the 'you', i.e., on God.[72] The link to Habakkuk should not be a diversion; it is quoted by Origen in this regard in *De Principiis*, and Athanasius' use of the reference in *In illud Omnia* refers to both cherubim and seraphim.[73] [73]It, therefore, appears that there is good reason to read the Sanctus as an invocation of the heavenly worship, perhaps a theme to the fore for a former monastic like Sarapion.[74] On that basis, we need not rule out the Origenistic interpretation.

---

[69] See the observations of Gregory Dix on this point, Gregory Dix, 'Primitive Consecration Prayers' in *Theology* 37 (1938) 273–75. Dix is inclined to stretch the evidence here and see a single point of origin for the eucharistic Sanctus. I only observe the imagery. Dix's account is also reviewed by Johnson, *Prayers of Sarapion*, 208–10.

[70] As seen in Athanasius, *In illud Omnia* 6; and Clement of Alexandria, *Stromateis* 7.12

[71] Spinks, *Sanctus*, 89.

[72] Maxwell E. Johnson, 'The Baptismal Rite and Anaphora in the Prayers of Sarapion of Thmuis: An Assessment of a Recent "Judicious Reassessment"' in *Worship* 73, no. 2 (March 1999) 161–62. Taft offers a further riposte to Spinks' case: Robert F. Taft, 'The Interpolation of the Sanctus into the Anaphora: When and Where? A Review of the Dossier Part I' in *Orientalia Christiana Periodica* 57, no. 2 (1991) 281–308; and 'The Interpolation of the Sanctus into the Anaphora: When and Where? A Review of the Dossier Part II' in *Orientalia Christiana Periodica* 58, no. 1 (1992) 83–121.

[73] Maxwell E. Johnson, 'The Archaic Nature of the Sanctus, Institution Narrative, and Epiclesis of the Logos in the Anaphora Ascribed to Sarapion of Thmuis' in Paul F.Bradshaw (ed), *Essays on Early Eastern Eucharistic Prayers* (Liturgical Press, Collegeville, 1997) 82.

[74] Johnson, 'Assessment of a Recent "Judicious Reassessment"', 163

Spinks notes some similarity in the Sanctus-epiclesis unit with the invocations of the divine name in Egyptian Greek magical papyri from Jewish and Gnostic sources. The examples Spinks quotes give particular focus to the title 'Sabaoth' found in the Sanctus, followed by an invocation for power to issue forth and to come and fill the offering. However, Spinks suggests these are only functional parallels rather than literary sources.[75]

It is possible that the text of Sarapion utilizes the image, taken from Origen, of the Son and of the Spirit as the seraphim joining the praise of the Father, as the anaphora calls upon the Father to send them as 'Power' and 'Participation' to fill the 'living sacrifice… the unbloody offering'. This is clearly a speculative interpretation, that is very open to an Arian interpretation.[76]

While we have seen the possibility of Athanasian influence in the use of the terms δύναμις and μετάληψις, the usage of them might mix his pro-Nicene theology with older Origenistic – and even Gnostic – ideas. This is perhaps why we find in the later development of **MK** that τῆς σῆς δυνάμεως καὶ τῆς σῆς μεταλήψεως has disappeared and been replaced by τῆς παρα σου εὐλογίας and 'face' has become 'faces'. The sense of what might have been an early Trinitarian invocation is lost, and a move is made away from Origen's picture of the Trinity in response to the final dominance of Athanasius and possible Syrian influences. Nevertheless, this may mean we have a transitional text.

Reviewing this debate, McGowan suggests much of the case Farag makes depends on whether Athanasius's theology is innovative or conservative, and argues for a conservativism in the liturgical texts at the least.[77] The approach to the seraphim suggest there is some mixing of older ideas with the pro-Nicene theology of Athanasius present in this passage, but nonetheless caution is necessary in how much confidence may be placed in any conclusions reached here. Nevertheless, there are

---

75 Spinks, *Sanctus*, 91–93.
76 cf. Rowan D. Williams, 'Angels Unawares: Heavenly Liturgy and Earthly Theology in Alexandria' in *Studia Patristica* 30 (Peeters, Louvain, 1997) 351–59.
77 McGowan, *Eucharistic Epicleses*, 74.

grounds for Farag's conclusion to favour the Athanasian interpretation of 'power' as the Son, and the language used not simply being a result of Syrian influences.

The Λογος Epiclesis

God of truth, let your holy Word come upon this bread in order that the bread may become body of the Word, and upon this cup in order that the cup may become blood of truth.

Ἐπιδημησάτω θεὲ τῆς ἀληθείας ὁ ἅγιος σου λόγος ἐπὶ τὸν ἄρτον τοῦτον, ἵνα γένηται ὁ ἄρτος σῶμα τοῦ λόγου, καὶ ἐπὶ τὸ ποτήριον τοῦτο, ἵνα γένηται τὸ ποτήριον αἷμα τῆς ἀληθείας.

This sentence is perhaps part of the Sacramentary that has attracted most attention. In context, it follows an extended Institution Narrative, and is followed by a petition for the fruits of communion. It stands unique amongst extant anaphoral epicleses in explicitly invoking the λόγος.[78] Here we will explore how this invocation may preserve some primitive ideas, and what it might have meant in the light of the thought of Athanasius.

Brock has made a convincing case for the antiquity of 'come' as the verb of invocation in the epiclesis in the Syrian tradition, with 'send' as a later development.[79] It must be shown whether this mirrors wider development. Nevertheless, the verb here is distinctive. Where 'come' is found in sources in Greek, such as **BAS** and the *Acts of Thomas*, the verb is normally ἔρχομαι, or one of its compound forms. The verb used here, ἐπιδημέω, whilst it can include 'come' within its range of meanings, carries the more specific sense of 'come home', 'come dwell', 'come to rest in', 'come to reside in'. This does convey similar tones to the combination

---

[78]   Robert F. Taft, 'From Logos to Spirit: On the Early History of the Epiclesis' in Andreas Heinz and Heinrich Rennings (ed), *Gratias Agamus: Studien Zum Eucharistischen Hochgebet: Für Balthasar Fischer*, Pastoralliturgische Reihe in Verbindung Mit Der Zeitschrift 'Gottesdienst' (Herder, Freiburg, 1992) 495.
[79]   See, as noted above, Brock, 'Invocations'.

of verbs 'come, rest and dwell' found in the East Syrian tradition, but with the exception of **A&M**, the extant texts are later.[80] In the case of **A&M**, the history of the epiclesis is sufficiently disputed to leave its early form unclear.[81] It is thus difficult to accept on the grounds of the verb alone that this epiclesis is primitive.

It is not obvious that an invocation of the λόγος was a common part of the Egyptian liturgical tradition. **MK** invokes the Holy Spirit, in an extended form, recounting the Spirit's role in salvation history. There is evidence that an epiclesis invoking the Spirit was known in Egypt before the end of the fourth century. Theodoret of Cyrus records Peter II, Athanasius' immediate successor as bishop of Alexandria, denouncing the Arians and referring to the 'holy altar… where we call on the coming of the Holy Spirit'.[82] Likewise at the very beginning of the fifth century in the Second Paschal Letter of Theophilus of Alexandria, preserved in Jerome's Latin translation, there is a reference that suggests the agent of the consecration is understood to be the Spirit:[83]

> Panemque Dominicum, quo Salvatoris Corpus ostenditur, et quem frangimus in sanctificationem nostri: et sacrum calicem… per invocationem et adventum Sancti Spiritus sanctificari.

The value of these sources is questionable. Theophilus makes his reference in the midst of a denunciation of Origen. Having previously been an Origenist, he became a strong opponent following threats to his authority from his monks. As such, it seems that this might be a politically motivated statement, and as a result may actually highlight

---

[80] Bryan D. Spinks, 'The Consecratory Epiklesis in the Anaphora of St. James' in *Studia Liturgica* 11, no. 1 (1976) 26.

[81] McGowan, *Eucharistic Epicleses*, 51–53; Paul F. Bradshaw and Maxwell E. Johnson, *The Eucharistic Liturgies* (SPCK, London, 2012) 39–41.

[82] *Ecclesiastical History IV*, 19. ET. Peter II was bishop from 373-380

[83] Jerome, *Ep.* 98,13. PL22.801. This is commonly dated to c. 402. ET: 'The Bread of the Lord, which is shown to be the Body of the Saviour and which we break for our sanctification; and the sacred cup… are sanctified by the invocation and coming of the Holy Spirit.'

a recent change, rather than an historic tradition.[84] Theodoret's history is written to demonstrate the defeat of the Arians, and as such is only a mid-fifth century source for the use of a pneumatic epiclesis, and does not necessarily reflect accurately Peter's practice.[85]

Whilst there is no explicit example of a λόγος epiclesis in earlier record, there is a tradition of sacramental theology that closely associates the λόγος with the consecration of the elements, without any of it providing clear evidence of a corresponding liturgical expression. The following examples suggest the possibility that Sarapion's epiclesis preserves an earlier idea.[86]

The earliest such text can be found in the *First Apology* of Justin Martyr. Justin explains that the elements have been 'made the eucharist by the prayer of his word'.[87] It is not clear whether Justin has in mind an institution narrative or an epiclesis, or even the whole anaphora or pattern of praying. Nonetheless it seems to suggest the active agent is the λόγος. In one of his descriptions of the eucharist, Irenaeus writes 'the mingled cup and the manufactured bread receives the Word of God, and the eucharist of the blood and the body of Christ is made'.[88] Again, it is not possible to connect this idea to a liturgical form, but we continue to see the Word as the active agent.

Within the Egyptian tradition, this idea is also found. Clement of Alexandria, in a passage that begins as exegesis of 1 Timothy 5.23, moves to discuss the mixed cup of the eucharist, described as 'the mixture of both – of the water and of the Word – is called eucharist'.[89] Perhaps the most influential early theologian upon the world of Athanasius, as we have already seen, was Origen. In consideration of the effect of receiving the eucharist, he describes the eucharistic bread as 'that which is

---

[84] Johnson, 'Archaic Nature', 97

[85] cf. Johnson, *Prayers of Sarapion*, 243.

[86] See also ibid., 247–50.

[87] 'δι᾽ εὐχῆς λόγου τοῦ παρ᾽ αὐτοῦ'; *Apology* I,66,2. PE, p.70; ET: ANF 1, p.185.

[88] 'τὸ κεκραμένον ποτήριον, καὶ ὁ γεγονὼς ἄρτος ἐμιδέχεται τὸν λόγον τοῦ Θεοῦ, καὶ γίνεται ἡ εὐχαριστία σῶμα Χριστοῦ'; *Adversus Haereses* V.2.3. PG7 1125B5; ET: ANF 1, p.528.

[89] 'ἡ δὲ ἀμφοῖν αὖθις κρᾶσις, ποτοῦ τε καὶ Λόγου, εὐχαριστία κέκληται'; *Paedagogus* II.2. PG8 412A1; ET: ANF 2, p.242.

sanctified through the word of God and prayer'.[90]

Johnson seeks to highlight also the antiquity of the structure of Sarapion's epiclesis here by reference to the request for the bread to become the σῶμα τοῦ λόγου. Johnson suggests this parallels Origen's description of the consecrated eucharistic bread as 'the bread which God the Logos says is his body is the Logos himself as food of souls'.[91]

Turning to the later work of the fifth century Cyril of Alexandria, who was writing when we can be fairly confident of the presence of a pneumatic epiclesis in the anaphora, we still find a strong sense of the λόγος as the prime agent of the consecration. Gebremedhin suggests that 'Cyril regards Christ as the living and active agent… in the consecration and conversion of the elements.'[92] In his *Letter to Tiberius the Deacon*, Cyril writes, 'But we believe that the bringing of gifts celebrated in the churches are hallowed, blessed and perfected by Christ.'[93] Gebremedhin, whilst acknowledging that we cannot be sure that Cyril attributed no consecratory function to the Spirit, observes that Cyril makes almost no reference to it,[94] and instead suggests that, for Cyril, the eucharistic liturgy was

'a cultic prolongation of the Incarnation of the Logos… This emphasis is evident in Cyril's interpretation of the epiclesis, in which Christ is given a prominent place. It is this theme of the centrality of the Word made flesh as vivifier of man through the Eucharist which Cyril elaborates'.[95]

---

[90] ἁγιαζόμινον διὰ λόγου θεοῦ καὶ ἐντεύξεως'; *Commentary on Matthew* XI.14. PG13 948D1-2; ET: ANF 10, p.443.

[91] *Panis iste, quem deus verbum corpus suum esse fatetur, verbum est nutritorium animarum*'; In *Matth. Ser.* 85. GCS 38 p. 196; ET: Patrick Jacquemont, 'Origen', in Willy Rordorf (ed), *The Eucharist of the Early Christians* (Liturgical Press, Collegeville, 1978), 187. See Johnson, *Prayers of Sarapion*, 249–52.

Ezra Gebremedhin, *Life-Giving Blessing: An Inquiry into the Eucharistic Devotion of Cyril of Alexandria*, Studia Doctrinae Christianae Upsaliensia 17 (Acta Universitatis Upsaliensis,

[92] Uppsala, 1977) 65.

[93] PG76, 1097C10, ET as given in ibid., 64.

[94] Ibid.

[95] Ibid., 70.

These parallels suggest that Sarapion is not innovating here. However, it is a separate question to understand how this might have been understood in light of the theological development. Botte, as we noted above, was convinced this collection was the work of a later pneumatomachian, and suggested that this epiclesis was one of the clear signs of that heresy. The flaws in the other arguments for this position above were noted above.

We have seen a theological presentation of the work of the λόγος in the eucharist present before and after the time of the Sacramentary. Turning to Athanasius, we find such a close association between the λόγος and the Spirit, that 'an epiclesis of the Logos necessarily involves the Spirit also.'[96] Cuming and Johnson each cite a number of passages from **Ad Sarap** to illustrate this point:[97]

the Spirit was in the Word.[98]
the Spirit is the anointing and the seal by whom and in whom the Word anoints and seals all things [99]

For there is nothing which is not brought into being and actualized through the Word in the Spirit.[100]

When the Spirit again testified to Paul, it was Christ himself who spoke in him, so that the testimony which came from the Spirit was the Word's. Thus also when the Word visited the holy virgin Mary, the Spirit came to her with him, and the Word in the Spirit formed the body[101]

The Father creates all things through the Word in the Spirit. For where

---

[96]   Cuming, 'Thmuis', 573.
[97]   Johnson, Prayers of Sarapion, 236; Cuming, 'Thmuis', 573.
[98]   **Ad Sarap** 2.15.2.
[99]   **Ad Sarap** 1.23.6.
[100] **Ad Sarap** 1.31.2.
[101] **Ad Sarap** 1.31.12.

the Word is, there also is the Spirit, and the things created through the Word have their strength to exist through the Spirit from the Word.[102]

This list is not comprehensive. On this basis I conclude that this epiclesis preserves an ancient association of the sanctification of the eucharistic elements by the λόγος, while also being intimately linked to the later invocations of the Spirit in the close relationship Athanasius describes between λόγος and Spirit. Similar questions arise in respect of the epiclesis in the prayer of blessing of the water, to which we now turn.

The Baptismal Prayers

Look now from heaven and gaze upon these waters and fill them with holy spirit. Let your inexpressible word come to be in them…And as your only-begotten word, when he descended upon the waters of the Jordan made them holy, so also now let him descend into these. Let him make them holy and spiritual in order that those who are baptized may no longer be flesh and blood but spiritual and able to give worship to you.

ἔφιδε νῦν ἐκ τοῦ οὐρανοῦ καὶ ἐπίβλεψον ἐπὶ τὰ ὕδατα ταῦτα καὶ πλήρωσον αὐτὰ πνεύματος ἁγίου. ὁ ἀρρητός σου λόγος ἐν αὐτοῖς γενέσθω... καὶ ὡς κατελθὼν ὁ μονογενής σου λόγος ἐπὶ τὰ ὕδατα τοῦ Ἰορδάνου ἅγια ἀπέδειξεν, οὕτω καὶ νῦν ἐν τούτοις κατερχέσθω καὶ ἅγια καὶ πνευματικὰ ποιησάτω πρὸς τὸ μηκέτι σάρκα καὶ αἷμα εἶναι τοὺς βαπτιζομένους, ἀλλὰ πνευματικοὺς καὶ δυναμένους προσκυνεῖν σοὶ

We have said much already about the close association of the Spirit and the λόγος in relation to the second epiclesis. Here again, it is the λόγος invoked, but here, unlike the second epiclesis of the anaphora, alongside the Spirit. Nevertheless, we can also see a link back to the form of the first epiclesis of the anaphora, as the Spirit is here invoked to 'fill' the

---

[102] **Ad Sarap** 2.14.1.

waters, similar to the petition in the anaphora for the elements be filled with power and participation. The relationship between the λόγος and the Spirit that we saw spelt out in the references in **Ad Sarap** is presented here liturgically. Whilst it is the λόγος who is the primary actor, to paraphrase Athanasius, 'the Spirit comes with him'.[103]

Again we can see that the liturgical text is not without parallel. In Cyril of Jerusalem's *Procatechesis*, we find the candidates for baptism being told 'Then you may enjoy the Christ-bearing waters in all their fragrance [ἀπολαύσητε Χριστοφόρων ἐχόντων εὐωδίαν].'[104] We may see both a parallel to this epiclesis, and to Athanasius' description of the Spirit as the fragrance of Christ [τὴν εὐωδίαν καὶ πνοὴν] in **Ad Sarap** 1.23.7, and the sense in which he suggests that anointing in the Spirit imparts to the one anointed that fragrance.

In John Chrysostom's *Catechesis*, a clear parallel may be found. Chrysostom writes,[105]

> And what happened in the case of our Master's body also happens in the case of your own. Although John appeared to be holding his body by the head, it was the divine Word which led his body down into the streams of Jordan and baptized him. [ὁ δὲ Θεὸς Λόγος εἰς τὰ Ἰορδάνεια ῥεῖθρα κατῆγε καὶ ἐβάπτιζε]

Chrysostom gives central place here to the descent of the λόγος into the water as agent of sanctification in Christian baptism.

In neither of these cases do we have any reason to believe there was an epiclesis of the λόγος present in the rite, either at Antioch or Jerusalem.[106] There is certainly reference to a common pool of imagery.[107] Jesus' baptism is the common early image to interpret Christian baptism

---

[103] cf. **Ad Sarap** 1.31.12.
[104] *Procatechesis* 15. PG33 357A11; ET: DBL p.29.
[105] *Catechesis* III.3.13. SC366 p. 222; ET: DBL p. 41. Clearly, Chrysostom is not concerned with the practicalities of the depth of the Jordan here.
[106] Johnson, *Prayers of Sarapion*, 128.
[107] cf. Brightman, 'Sacramentary (Pt.2)', 248.

in the East, rather than Romans 6. Likewise, the metaphor of 'fragrance' is Pauline, coming from 2 Corinthians 2.15. Nevertheless, as with the references to earlier eucharistic theology reflecting the action of the λόγος in the consecration of the elements, these parallels suggest that Sarapion is not innovating in the theology of his baptismal rite.

This theology, of the λόγος being the primary actor, is also found in prayers 8 and 10, where we find petitions that 'guided by your only-begotten word, he [the candidate] may give worship to you always and keep your commandments' and 'let your only-begotten word guide him to the bath... Let your holy word be present and let your holy Spirit be with him to drive away and cast out every temptation'. The latter quotation, from Prayer 10, highlights again the close relationship between λόγος and Spirit.

We have already described the linked role of the Spirit and the λόγος in Ad Sarap 1.23, where Athanasius describes the Spirit as unction and seal.[108] While, given the concerns which Johnson has raised with the unity of prayers 15-17 and 7-11 in a single rite, [109] it is difficult to say how this relates to the epiclesis over the water, it indicates how the close association of λόγος and Spirit runs throughout the whole Sacramentary, and is not limited only to these prayers containing clear invocations.

The Prayer for the Ordination of Presbyters

Master, God of the heavens, Father of your only-begotten, we extend (our) hand(s) upon this man and we pray that the Spirit of truth may come to him. Graciously give him insight and knowledge and a good heart. Let divine Spirit come to be in him that he might be able to govern your people, to act as an ambassador of your divine words, and to reconcile your people to you, the uncreated God. From the spirit of Moses you graciously gave holy Spirit to the elect ones. Distribute holy Spirit also to this one from the Spirit of the only-begotten for the

---

108 Spinks, 'Judicious Reassessment', 268.
109 Johnson, *Prayers of Sarapion*, 85–87, 89–91, 124–26; see also Johnson, 'Assessment of a Recent "Judicious Reassessment", 141–55

gift of wisdom and knowledge and right faith, that he may be able to
serve you with a pure conscience. Through your only-begotten Jesus
Christ, through whom (be) to you the glory and the power in holy
Spirit both now and to all the ages of ages. Amen.

Τὴν χεῖρα ἐκτείνομεν δέσποτα θεὲ τῶν οὐρανῶν πάτερ τοῦ μονογενοῦς
σου ἐπὶ τὸν ἄνθρωπον τοῦτον καὶ δεόμεθα ἵνα τὸ πνεῦμα τῆς ἀληθείας
ἐπιδημήσῃ αὐτῷ· φρόνησιν αὐτῷ χάρισαι καὶ γνῶσιν καὶ καρδίαν ἀγαθήν·
γενέσθω ἐν αὐτῷ πνεῦμα θεῖον πρὸς τὸ δύνασθαι αὐτὸν οἰκονομῆσαι
τὸν λαόν σου καὶ πρεσβεύειν τὰ θεῖά σου λόγια καὶ καταλλάξαι τὸν λαόν
σου σοὶ τῷ ἀγενήτῳ θεῷ. ὁ χαρισάμενος ἀπὸ τοῦ πνεύματος τοῦ Μωσέως
ἐπὶ τοὺς ἐκλελεγμένους πνεῦμα ἅγιον, μέρισον καὶ τῷδε πνεῦμα ἅγιον
ἐκ τοῦ πνεύματος τοῦ μονογενοῦς εἰς χάριν σοφίας καὶ γνώσεως καὶ
πίστεως ὀρθῆς, ἵνα δυνηθῇ σοι ὑπηρετῆσαι ἐν καθαρᾷ συνειδήσει· διὰ
τοῦ μονογενοῦς σου Ἰησοῦ Χριστοῦ, δι᾽ οὗ σοὶ ἡ δόξα καὶ τὸ κράτος ἐν
ἁγίῳ πνεύματι καὶ νῦν καὶ εἰς τοὺς σύμπαντας αἰῶνας τῶν αἰώνων. ἀμήν.

Compared to the other prayers we have considered, and in the
Sacramentary in general, the approach to the Holy Spirit in this prayer is
different. It is also a prayer that is hard to place within the context of the
prayers around it. Its concerns differ from the prayers for the ordination
of deacons (12) and the bishop (14), in that this prayer seems to favour
a theology where the act of election is more significant, whereas they
favour the act of prayer itself. This is illustrated by the lack of reference
to an election here and the sense in which the new presbyter is already
a presbyter, and instead a request for the gifts needed for the office. In
contrast, in the prayer for the bishop, we find 'Through him [Christ]
you elected the apostles, appointing holy bishops from generation to
generation. Make this one also a living bishop'. Similarly, for deacons,
we find 'You elected bishops and presbyters and deacons… Appoint also
this one a deacon of your catholic church.'[110] Comparison with liturgical

---

[110] cf. Johnson, *Prayers of Sarapion*, 148–50.

practice elsewhere in the period is limited, as this is the only liturgical text, besides the *Apostolic Tradition* and its derivatives, that dates from before the seventh century.[111]

Another suggestion of the antiquity of this prayer is given by the reference to preaching. In Socrates' *Historia Ecclesiastica*, he notes that, after Arius, no presbyter was allowed to preach at Alexandria, a restriction also noted by Sozomen.[112] We cannot be sure this applied at Thmuis as well, nor when the restriction began at Alexandria, so this does not provide a firm dating to the prayer, but may provide an indication.[113]

Finally, we may see a further sign of this antiquity in that it seems to place the presbyters in a position to govern (οἰκονομέω) the church. It appears that the authority of the presbyterate in Egypt, at least in terms of authority to appoint their own bishop, was greater prior to the Council of Nicaea.[114] Bradshaw suggests that the verb should more accurately be translated in terms of being a steward, and notes that the parallel drawn with the spirit of Moses is not a parallel of offices but of 'God's action in sharing the Spirit'.[115] This seems to be an unusual translation of the verb, and the interpretation of governance does not hinge on the Mosaic imagery.[116] These factors, along with the literary links which Johnson identifies to place this in the first stratum of the Sacramentary, lead us to conclude that this prayer is early.

It is also interesting to note, in light of Botte's suggestion that the document was edited by a pneumatomachian, that it is the Spirit that is invoked, and not the λόγος. Clearly, if this document were the work of an editor who was deliberately minimizing the role of the Spirit, we would

---

[111] Paul F. Bradshaw, *Rites of Ordination: Their History and Theology* (SPCK, London, 2014) 58. As Bradshaw notes, we do not know how the Apostolic Tradition prayers relate to actual usage. Bradshaw elsewhere suggests there is no evidence for any literary interdependence: Paul F. Bradshaw, *Ordination Rites of the Ancient Churches of East and West* (Pueblo, New York, 1990) 5

[112] *Historia Ecclesiastica* 5.22. ET: NPNF2-02 p. 132. See also Sozomen, *Historia Ecclesiastica* 7.19. ET: NPNF2-03, p. 390.

[113] Bradshaw, *Rites of Ordination*, 80.

[114] Johnson, *Prayers of Sarapion*, 152

[115] Bradshaw, *Ordination Rites*, 64

[116] Johnson, *Prayers of Sarapion*, 153

not expect a prayer to survive in this form. Instead we have implications of the Spirit as the 'Spirit of truth', of knowledge, of reconciliation, and 'of wisdom and knowledge and right faith'. Clearly, some of these themes were part of the *Formelgut* from which such prayers were formed, especially as they are largely scriptural ideas. Nonetheless, none would be out of place in the gifts that Athanasius would attribute to the work of the Spirit.

Conclusion

The Sacramentary of Sarapion is not a uniform collection systematically composed and refined by a single hand. However, this examination shows that it reflects an Egyptian and an Athanasian theology of the Holy Spirit. evidenced in the links back to the thought of Origen we have seen in the construction of the first epiclesis of the anaphora. The close associations between the λόγος and the Spirit exhibited by the use of λόγος in the second epiclesis and in the epiclesis over the water, indicate the influence of Athanasius' theology and the close relationship between the Son and the Spirit central to the argument of **Ad Sarap**. The first epiclesis exhibits some indicators of Athanasius' influence; as a result, I have shown that there is a possibility that the use of δύναμις and μετάληψις reflects the use of the terms in relation to the Son and the Spirit respectively. Finally, the prayer for the ordination of presbyters shows that the final redactor of the collection cannot have been a pneumatomachian, as has been claimed.

3

The Cappadocian Fathers and the Anaphoras of St. Basil

This chapter will seek to explore whether there is a relationship between ideas concerning the Holy Spirit in the doctrinal writings of Basil the Great, especially his treatise *De Spiritu Sancto*, and in the liturgical matter of the same period, with particular attention to the *Anaphora of St. Basil*. I will begin with a brief consideration of the situation in which Basil worked in order to be able to set the doctrinal texts in context. I will then consider the theology of the Spirit laid down in Basil's treatise. I will next analyze the evidence connecting Basil to the liturgical material, and attempt to understand what involvement he may have had, in what quickly becomes a complex picture. These two components will then be utilized to consider the extent to which we can see Basil's ideas in the text of the anaphora.

De Spiritu Sancto and Basil's Theology of the Holy Spirit

We must begin by noting, first, Basil never explicitly calls the Spirit 'God'; and second, it is impossible to consider Basil's theology without the context of political – both ecclesiastical and imperial – manoeuvring that he was involved in. [117] His theology must be seen in light of that context.

Basil and Politics

Unlike Athanasius, who has been characterized by the maxim *Athanasius*

---

[117] See Lewis Ayres, *Nicaea and Its Legacy: An Approach to Fourth-Century Trinitarian Theology* (Oxford University Press, Oxford, 2009) 216, 221.

contra mundum,[118] Basil was a man of alliances, albeit ones that shifted constantly. Ayres suggests,

> 'in his attempts at alliance-building Basil was creating an audience receptive to his theology, and in his theology Basil was shaping a vocabulary that would reflect his own evolving position whilst being persuasive to those he wished to bring into alliance.'[119]

This is not to suggest Basil compromised principles to win friends, but it indicates why he refrains from stating what seems the obvious conclusion of his work, that the Holy Spirit is God. In Ayres' assessment, Basil's constant problems in building these alliances were that under the Emperor Valens, the Homoian camp had political support; and that personal conflicts and ambitions were as problematic as doctrine.[120] On the first count it is telling that the triumph of the pro-Nicene camp comes only with the succession of Theodosius.[121] On the latter, we can note the difficulty Basil had with breaking off his relationship with his ascetic mentor, Eustathius of Sebaste, when he could not be convinced to join the pro-Nicene camp, along with the renewed vigour shown by Basil in light of the relationship he begins to form with Amphilochius, the bishop of Iconium to whom he addresses **DSS** and writes a number of letters.[122] Further, in loyalty to Meletius regarding the see of Antioch, Basil loses potential support from Rome and Alexandria in the doctrinal conflict.[123]

Basil and Pneumatology

Though by no means the only place where he writes about the Spirit, **DSS** is Basil's clearest statement of his own theological position. We see

---

[118] Cf. C.S. Lewis, 'Preface in John Behr (ed), *On the Incarnation, by Athanasius*, Popular Patristics Series, no. 44a (St Vladimir's Seminary Press, Yonkers, N.Y, 2011), 16. But note also his alliance with Marcellus of Ancyra, see Edwards, *Catholicity and Heresy*, 108–9.
[119] Ayres, *Nicaea*, 222.
[120] Ibid., 222ff.
[121] See ibid., 240–43.
[122] See Rousseau, *Basil*, 239, 261–69; Ayres, *Nicaea*, 225–26.
[123] Ayres, *Nicaea*, 226–29.

something of its development in **Adv Eun** and in Ep. 233-235, written to Amphilochius, and it is clear that this is a process of evolution, responding to the differing challenges he faces. With this in mind, it seems most appropriate to focus our attention primarily on **DSS**.

DSS splits into three major parts, enclosed between prologue and epilogue. The first and last parts, chapters 2–8 and 25–29, are primarily treatises on the proper use of prepositions in relation to the each of the persons of the Trinity. Basil argues that the choice of such prepositions in Scripture is sufficiently inconsistent that we cannot use it to describe the relations of the Persons. The other major part, comprising the centrepiece of the treatise, is a series of theses, giving Basil's own view, and his refutations of his critics' positions. Whilst the work on prepositions tells us little of Basil's pneumatology, the combinations of these theses with the alternative explanations given in the refutations is revealing.[124]

Haykin argues that chapter 9 should stand apart from the second part, possibly originally as a separate composition, because it is less polemic and reflects distinctive themes, particularly in not referencing the baptismal formula.[125] It is possible that in origin it is an independent composition, but if characterized as the first thesis of the second part, as Hildebrand proposes, it perhaps offers some common ground before the first refutation in chapter 10, and therefore is at home in the document as a whole.[126]

The discussion of prepositions apart, Basil is principally undertaking an exegesis of the baptismal formula and of 1 Corinthians 12.3. As Haykin observes, his method is not that of modern exegesis, and as a result we cannot engage with it in that manner; instead, for Basil, exegesis is a function of the experience of the Church, with soteriology always central. [127]

---

[124] Stephen M Hildebrand, *The Trinitarian Theology of Basil of Caesarea: A Synthesis of Greek Thought and Biblical Interpretation*. (Catholic University of America Press, Washington, 2009)
[125] Haykin, *Spirit of God*, 106–7. Haykin would also see part of the second treatise on prepositions incorporated into the central part, and would regard chapters 28-29 as a separate unit (pp. 108-113). As he acknowledges the difficulty of then making sense of this unit, the model we have given, from Hildebrand, seems more coherent.
[126] Hildebrand, *Trinitarian Theology*, 180.
[127] Haykin, *Spirit of God*, 116. This is only unfamiliar to modern, post-Enlightenment criticism.

Therefore, we must turn to soteriology to understand Basil's pneumatology. It is clear that, for Basil, salvation is coming to knowledge of truth, that 'as if we were eyes kept in darkness, [God leads]… us up to the great light of truth, accustoming us to it little by little.'[128] In this way, moral impurity is effectively one form of ignorance. This is not just a repetition of Hellenistic ideas, but the use of them to express 'a Christian solution to the problems of ignorance and sin.'[129] In this way, Basil, in **DSS** 14, is interpreting the whole of the economy of salvation as the movement from darkness into light. Similar illumination imagery is used from Isaiah 9.2 and John 1.5, along with the sense of the Law as a 'shadow of things to come' Basil quotes from Hebrews 10.1, not just from Hellenistic sources.[130]

It is this that allows Basil to place his focus on 1 Corinthians 12.3. It is in the Spirit that one gains knowledge of the Son, and thus is able to confess Jesus as Lord. He also emphasizes the choice of preposition here – that it is ἐν rather than δία, that is used.[131] Just as the Spirit is the one who reveals the Son, Basil has no doubts that it is through the Son that one comes to know the Father.[132] In understanding the Spirit as the Spirit of knowledge, mediating salvation and illumination in this manner, for Basil this necessitates the Spirit individual and substantial membership of the Godhead, and intimate relationship with the Son and, subsequently, the Father.

If this was the entirety of Basil's argument, then it would be hard to see it as more than speculative theology, particularly with his use of Greek philosophy. However, he roots it in the practice of the Church too, in particular in baptism. While it is never obvious whether Basil is quoting Matthew 28.19, or established liturgical custom, it is not hugely

---

The continuity Basil sees between Scripture and Tradition and the question of soteriology are common to all ancient commentators.

[128] **DSS** 14,33. Here we see a clear reference to Plato's cave metaphor from *The Republic*, Book VII

[129] Hildebrand, *Trinitarian Theology*, 175.

[130] **DSS** 14,33.

[131] **DSS** 18,47. See Haykin, *Spirit of God*, 125–29.

[132] cf. John 14.7.

significant which of these alternatives he has in mind. It is perhaps the combined effect that makes it 'the immovable foundation of trinitarian theology.'[133]

For Basil, baptism in the name of the Father alone would be insufficient, because without the Son, the Father is unknowable. Similarly, baptism in the name of the Father and the Son is still ineffective, as without the Holy Spirit, *per* 1 Corinthians 12.3, one cannot call Jesus 'Lord'. Thus, the baptismal formula frames the understanding of the Spirit in this epistemic action. Basil takes this and turns it into what Hildebrand calls one of his 'most powerful arguments for the Spirit's divinity; the Spirit is divine, because he epistemically unites the baptized to the Father through the Son.'[134]

Basil suggests that baptism is the most complete participation in the Spirit for the believer, so that 'The Spirit illuminates those who have been cleansed from every stain and makes them spiritual by means of communion with himself.'[135] Nevertheless, the Spirit 'is not participated in all at once but shares his energy in "proportion to faith".'[136] Thus baptism must be filled with faith to lead to salvation.[137]

Aside from this basic characterization of the Spirit, centred as we have seen on his epistemic relation to the Son and revealed in the baptismal formula, Basil highlights a number of other features of the Spirit: righteousness; beyond circumscription; infinite in intelligence, power and greatness; immeasurable by time; source of all holiness; inspiration of virtue; 'inaccessible in nature, but approachable in goodness.'[138] He emphasizes the equal role of the Spirit as creator, as the perfecter of that work, while the Father is the cause and the Son the maker[139]

---

[133] Haykin, *Spirit of God*, 129
[134] Hildebrand, *Trinitarian Theology*, 178
[135] **DSS** 9,23.
[136] **DSS** 9,22.
[137] See also **DSS** 15,35.
[138] **DSS** 9,22. See Hildebrand, *Trinitarian Theology*, 181.
[139] **DSS** 16,38. The use of angels as the tool in showing this seems not to be an attempt to limit the extent of the conclusions, merely a satisfactory abstraction.

Basil and the Anaphoras that bear his name

Basilian authorship cannot be ascribed to the anaphoras which bear his name as it can to his systematic works. Only a brief survey of the breadth of the debate is possible here.

(a)   Basil the Arranger of Prayers

The only contemporary source which we have to indicate that Basil had a specific interest in the liturgy and the composition of the texts for it, lies in the funeral oration Gregory of Nazianzus gave for him. Basil is described as being involved in and supporting 'the arrangement of prayers'.[140] This phrase is a translation of 'εὐχῶν διατάξεις';[141] the sense of which includes the composition of new prayers and the revision of the liturgy around them. Yet, that begs the question as to whether this was yet abnormal at this stage of the fourth century, and whether every bishop composed, or even extemporized, a eucharistic prayer. There can be no doubt that the fourth century was more restrictive in this regard than early periods, but some freedom seemingly continued.[142]

Basil himself makes little comment on liturgy, or liturgical ordering. In **DSS**, he acknowledges that there has been a process of development and redaction in the liturgy, and that nothing complete was handed down from the apostolic age, saying,

> Which saint has left us a scriptural account of the words of the epiclesis at the manifestation of the bread of the eucharist and the cup of blessing? We are not satisfied with the words that the Apostle or the

---

[140] Or. 43.34.2, ET: NPNF2-07 p.407.

[141] PG36 541C4.

[142] Cuming argues that the freedom was quite curtailed by this period, but still extant. See John R. K. Fenwick, *The Anaphoras of St. Basil and St. James* (Pontificum Institutum Orientale, Rome, 1992) *Orientalia Christiana Analecta* 240, 21–22; Cuming, 'Pseudonymity', 536–37. Earlier scholarship would tend to argue that there was no such freedom. See, for example, S. Salaville, *Liturgies Orientales: Notions Générales Éléments Principaux* (Bloud et Gay, Paris, 1932) 60. On this question, see Allan Bouley, *From Freedom to Formula: The Evolution of the Eucharistic Prayer from Oral Improvisation to Written Texts*, Studies in Christian Antiquity 21 (Catholic University of America Press, Washington, DC, 1981). Chapter 5 (pp. 217-253) is of particular pertinence to Basil's situation.

Gospel mentions, but we add other words before and after theirs…[143]

While this text could imply Basil's involvement in the creation of the 'other words', that interpretation assumes much – Basil gives no more than an awareness of the existence of a process. It does not, of course, give us the degree to which Basil made changes, within the existing tradition, according to his context.

(b) Early References

While we have limited primary evidence of Basil's personal involvement, the tradition of an anaphora attributed to him dates back to at least the sixth or seventh century. The references are sparse enough that we can say no more than that there was a liturgy known widely by his name.

This attribution may be found in the writing of Leontius of Byzantium, who in c. 543 claims its use in the time of Theodore of Mopsuestia (that is, c.425-430);[144] in a letter attributed to Peter the Deacon (died c. 605), which cites a passage found in some recensions of the anaphora but not universally;[145] and in the canons of the Council 'in Trullo' of 692.[146] Similarly, one of the earliest manuscripts of the Byzantine recension of the anaphora, the eighth century Codex Barberini Gr 336, contains an attribution to Basil, though placed alongside the Prayer of the Proscomide rendering the whole attribution doubtful.[147]

The so-called 'Tradition of Proclus of Constantinople' (d.446)

---

[143] **DSS** 27, 66.e

[144] *Adv. Incorrupticolas et Nestor.*, 19. PG86 1368C.

[145] *Liber de Incarnatione et Gratia*, VIII. PL62 90C. This letter is also preserved in the corpus of works of Fulgentius as Ep. XVI (seu liber Petri Diaconi et aliorum qui in causa fidei Graecis ex Oriente Roman missi fuerunt) VII.25. PL65 449D..

[146] Canon XXXII includes 'For also James, the brother, according to the flesh, of Christ our God, to whom the throne of the church of Jerusalem first was entrusted, and Basil, the Archbishop of the Church of Cæsarea, whose glory has spread through all the world, when they delivered to us directions for the mystical sacrifice in writing, declared that the holy chalice is consecrated in the Divine Liturgy with water and wine.' ET: NPNF2-14, p. 380. The context is a prohibition of an unmixed chalice.

[147] LEW p.319. For comment, see Robert F. Taft, *The Great Entrance* (Pontifico Istituto Orientale, Rome, 2004) Orientalia Christian Analecta 200, 360–69; Fenwick, *Basil and James*, 23–24.

suggests that Basil inherited a longer form of the anaphora and on pastoral grounds abbreviated it.[148] Scholarship in the early twentieth century largely presumed the authenticity of this claim, and thus that **ByzBAS** was the longer form, and **E-BAS** Basil's abbreviation. The work attributed to Proclus has been shown to be a sixteenth century forgery, and therefore the development it describes should be ignored, and it cannot provide evidence for the involvement of Basil himself. [149]

(c) Modern Scholarship

In the modern scholarship, the question of the possible involvement of Basil is intimately caught up with theories as to the interdependence of the different recensions. We shall survey the differing approaches, beginning with the work of Engberding, which has become the archetypal model against which other theories are referenced.[150]

A student of Baumstark, Engberding was, by reference to his mentor's laws of liturgical evolution, suspicious of the case made by Pseudo-Proclus.[151] By the principles proposed by Baumstark, one would not expect abbreviation but expansion. Engberding categorized the different recensions by geographical groupings, and posited a hypothetical common source to the longer recensions which he labelled Ω.[152] He also posited an *Urgestalt* behind all the editions, and that Basil took this *Ur-*

---

[148]   *Tractatus de Traditione Divinae Missae*. PG65 849B-852B. The specific reference comes towards the end of the text.

[149]   Anne Vorhes McGowan, 'The Basilian Anaphoras: Rethinking the Question' in Maxwell E. Johnson (ed), *Issues in Eucharistic Praying in East and West: Essays in Liturgical and Theological Analysis* (Liturgical Press, Collegeville, 2011) 228–29. The demonstration of the forgery is the work of F.J. Leroy, 'Proclus, "de Traditione Divinae Missae": Un Faux de C. Palaeocappa' in *Orientalia Christiana Periodica* 28 (1962) 288–99.

[150]   McGowan, 'Basilian Anaphoras', 261. This is not a comprehensive survey. Such work is done effectively by McGowan, and also, although written before some of the most significant recent contributions, by D. Richard Stuckwisch, 'The Basilian Anaphoras' in Paul F. Bradshaw (ed), *Essays on Early Eastern Eucharistic Prayers* (Liturgical Press, Collegeville, 1997) 109–30.

[151]   While Engberding was influenced by Baumstark, we cannot, of course, adopt Baumstark's methodology uncritically. Note the discussion in Paul F. Bradshaw, *The Search for the Origins of Christian Worship* (2nd edn, SPCK, London, 2002) chap. 1; Robert F. Taft and Gabriele Winkler (eds), *Comparative Liturgy Fifty Years after Anton Baumstark (1872-1948), Rome, 25-29 September 1998*, Orientalia Christiana Analecta 265 (Pontificio Istituto Orientale, Rome, 2001).

[152]   That is to say as the common source to the Syriac, the Armenian and the Byzantine recensions.

BAS, and his redactions resulted in **Ω-BAS**. He considered **E-BAS** to be an independent redaction of **Ur-BAS**. His conclusions may be summarized by Figure 1. There was one significant limitation of Engberding's work, namely that he only considered the Preface, pre-Sanctus, Sanctus and post-Sanctus, and therefore did not examine a significant amount of the text.[153]

Figure 1: Engberding's Model

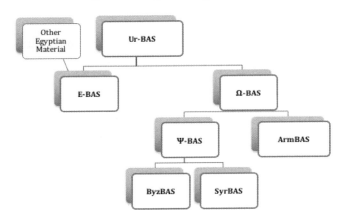

Engberding's conclusions must also be re-evaluated in light of the subsequent manuscript discoveries. In 1960, Doresse and Lanne published a critical edition of the Sahidic text of the Egyptian recension of the prayer.[154] This, through the accompanying essay by Capelle, led to widespread acceptance of an early date for this **ES-BAS**, and of this recension as relatively accurately reflecting the *Urtext*.[155] This does not rule out the

---

[153] McGowan, 'Basilian Anaphoras', 229–30. Figure 2 is freely adapted from similar charts in Hieronymus Engberding, *Das Eucharistische Hochgebet Der Basileiosliturgie: Textgeschichtliche Untersuchungen Und Kritische Ausgabe*, Theologie Der Christlichen Ostens 1 (Verlag Aschendorff, Munster, 1931) LXXXVII; and Fenwick, *Basil and James*, 308.

[154] J. Doresse, E. Lanne, and B. Capelle, *Un Témoin Archaïque de La Liturgie Copte de S. Basile. (En Annexe: Les Liturgies 'Basilennes' et Saint Basile)* (Publications Universitaires/Institut Orientaliste, Louvain, 1960).

[155] Ibid., I–II.

influence of Basil as a redactor for the Ω group.[156]

Fenwick's analysis completes the work of Engberding, analyzing the remainder of the anaphora in the same comparative manner.[157] His main distinctive conclusion is to highlight the interface with **JAS** in the development of both anaphoral traditions, suggesting a shared *Urtext* that has much in common with **ES-BAS**. Again, this does not largely revise the hypothesis over the opportunities for Basil's influence, and indeed Fenwick has been criticized for insufficiently emphasizing the distinctively Egyptian elements within **E-BAS**.

For example, Todd Johnson looks at the Louvain manuscript that lies at the heart of Doresse and Lanne's edition of **E-BAS** as though it had nothing to do with the Basilian tradition, and finds significant indicators of an Egyptian background and several primitive characteristics. One feature he emphasizes is the unusual doxology, paralleled in other Egyptian anaphoras. Therefore we cannot underestimate the influence of the Egyptian source material assumed by Engberding.[158]

Two earlier scholars had made efforts to evidence the influence of Basil himself upon these anaphoras by exploring possible linguistic links between the euchological texts and his known writings, Bernard Capelle[159] and Boris Bobrinskoy.[160] Their work, based on the work of Engberding, provides two initial points of reference. First, Engberding claims, for Basil, doxology should be scriptural – on which Basil writes:

> When you glorify God, do not let your mind wander greatly here and there… but let it select from the sacred Scriptures.[161]

Second, Engberding identifies a preference for praise of the divine

---

[156] McGowan, 'Basilian Anaphoras', 230–32.
[157] Fenwick, *Basil and James*.
[158] Todd E. Johnson, 'Recovering Ägyptisches Heimatgut: An Exercise in Liturgical Methodology' in *Questions Liturgiques* 76 (1995) 192 *et passim*.
[159] In the aforementioned essay.
[160] Boris Bobrinskoy, 'Liturgie et Ecclésiologie Trinitaire de Saint Basile' in *Verbum Caro* 89 (1969): 1–32.
[161] *Constitutiones Monasticae* 1,2. PG31 1329A1-5; ET: Fenwick, *Basil and James*, 27.

economy over praise for creation. On this he sees parallels to the emphasis of passages in Basil's *Homilia in martyrem Iulittam* and his *Longer Rules*.[162]

Engberding's conclusions are weak. As to the first point, the authenticity of the *Constitutiones Monasticae* as a work of Basil is doubtful – in the introduction to his 1925 edition of Basil's *Ascetic Works*, Clarke suggests it is the work of later monastics living in the tradition of Basil's *Rules*, and not of the saint himself.[163] It is also omitted from Wagner's 1950 edition, presumably on the same basis.[164] Rousseau has observed the importance of Scripture throughout Basil's *Ascetica*,[165] and perhaps the view is consistent with Basil's generally high view of Scripture and the instructions he gives for worship in his *Longer Rules* XXXVII; but this only permits a limited label of 'Basiline'. Nevertheless, we may wish to note – albeit cautiously – Baumstark's 'law' suggests more use of Scripture in later liturgical texts irrespective of the author.[166] We shall come in more detail to Winkler's work in due course, but by placing **BAS** within a Syrian environment, she identifies that many of the scriptural allusions may have come through the canons of the Antiochene synods, not directly from Scripture.[167]

As to his second point, the context in which the cited remarks in the homily and the *Rules* are made is such that we would expect Basil to refer us to the οἰκονομία rather than to creation. A consideration of the *Hexaemeron* makes it difficult to see Basil as unconcerned with creation

---

[162] See *Homilia in martyrem Iulittam*, 7, PG31 253C and *Longer Rules*, PG913A. See Engberding, Hochgebet, LXXXV. Note also Fenwick's commentary, though Fenwick appears to confuse the two separate references which Engberding gives: see Fenwick, *Basil and James*, 27.

[163] W.K.L. Clarke (ed), *The Ascetic Works of Saint Basil* (SPCK, London, 1925) 36.

[164] M. Monica Wagner, *Ascetical Works of St. Basil* (Catholic University of America Press, Washington, DC, 1950).

[165] Rousseau, *Basil*, 194ff..

[166] Anton Baumstark, *Comparative Liturgy*, trans. F.L. Cross (A.R. Mowbray & Co., London, 1958) 59. As noted above, there is a limit as to how far these may be applied. However, given Engberding was a student of Baumstark, we might expect him to follow in his master's footsteps and express a greater corresponding caution.

[167] Gabriele Winkler, 'The Christology of the Anaphora of Basil in Its Various Redactions, with Some Remarks Concerning the Authorship of Basil' in Bryan D.Spinks (ed), *The Place of Christ in Liturgical Prayer: Trinity, Christology, and Liturgical Theology* (Liturgical Press, Collegeville, 2008) 114–17.

in doxology, being the focus of the work, although it also becomes clear that there is no strict divide in Basil's thought between the οἰκονομία and creation – the latter is a part of the former.[168]

Capelle focuses more than Engberding on linguistic similarities between **ByzBAS** and the remainder of the Basilian corpus. In the process he identifies one possible parallel to Athanasius in the preface, in language used of the Son, but since this is a single reference, it is easy to place too much emphasis on it.[169] Furthermore Basil was familiar with at least some of Athanasius' thought, such that integrating his ideas and language would be plausible – perhaps to prove orthodoxy to his neighbours.[170]

Capelle carries this study through the preface and into the pre- and post-Sanctus, and continues to find parallels to the works of Basil.[171] An example of his approach is given in the handling of a part of the recounting of the salvific economy between the Sanctus and the Institution Narrative. The anaphora has:

1	προφήτας ἐξαπέστειλας,
2	ἐποίησας δυνάμεις διὰ τῶν ἁγίων σου τῶν κατ' ἑκάστην γενεὰν καὶ γενεὰν εὐαρεστησάντων σοι...
3	νόμον ἔδωκας εἰς βοήθειαν
4	ἀγγέλους ἐπέστηκας φυλάκας

Capelle finds four points of comparison in the Basilian corpus. Firstly, in the *Longer Rules*, phrases 3,4 and 1 are repeated almost word for word.[172]

---

[168] *Hexaemeron*, PG 29 4-208; ET: FC46. On this, see Frances Margaret Young, *God's Presence: A Contemporary Recapitulation of Early Christianity* (Cambridge University Press, Cambridge, 2013) 92–145.
[169] Doresse, Lanne, and Capelle, *Témoin Archaïque*, 51–52.
[170] cf. Rousseau, *Basil*, 294–95.
[171] Doresse, Lanne, and Capelle, *Témoin Archaïque*, 56–63. The following example is explored on pp. 58-60.
[172] *Longer Rules* II,30. The main difference here in *Rules* seems to be to move some words into a different case and an extra descriptor in phrase 4. PG31 913C1-3.

Also, in **DSS**, we see the description of the divine economy as:[173]

Further, and more partial, comparison is made to Ep. 261,[174] and to Basil's fifth homily on the *Hexaemeron*.[175] The linguistic similarities are obvious, and make a strong case to associate Basil with the text.

A key criticism of the work of Capelle is that he goes no further than the post-Sanctus. Presumably this is in part because the comparative work of Engberding goes no further either. Bobrinskoy, in his study, extends the survey through into the institution narrative, the epiclesis and the intercessions, finding indicators of Basil's Christology, pneumatology and ecclesiology.[176] For instance, Bobrinskoy finds similarity within the intercessions to Basil's approach over the peace and unity of the Church, the place and understanding of the priesthood and the ascetic life, and the cosmic dimension to intercession.[177] Another criticism that may be levelled is that the comparison is only directly made to **ByzBAS** rather than to Ω-**BAS**. However, as later studies have shown, constructing an Ω text is non-trivial, and so comparison to a particular recension is more useful.

Fenwick reviews the contribution of Engberding, Capelle and Bobrinskoy, saying that 'together [they] present an impressive, and perhaps conclusive, case for believing that St Basil himself was the source of much of the material that distinguishes the anaphora of Ω-Basil from that of E-Basil.'[178] This conclusion is challenged by two of the most significant recent contributions to the debate concerning the origins of **BAS**, those of Budde and Winkler.

Budde's study focuses on the Egyptian elements within the prayer.[179]

---

[173] **DSS** 16,39; SC17 p.386 ll.5-8.

[174] PG32 969AB.

[175] PG29 108C.

[176] Bobrinskoy, 'Liturgie et Ecclésiologie'. His work is summarized by McGowan, 'Basilian Anaphoras', 232.

[177] Bobrinskoy, 'Liturgie et Ecclésiologie', 22.

[178] Fenwick, *Basil and James*, 28.

[179] Achim Budde, *Die Ägyptische Basilios-Anaphora: Text-Kommentar-Geschichte*, Jerusalemer Theologisches Forum 7 (Aschendorff, Münster, 2004). For a discussion of his argument in English, and the critiques of it, see McGowan, 'Basilian Anaphoras', 250–60. The consideration of it here is based on McGowan's summary.

By constructing a comparative edition of the different versions (Greek, Bohairic and Sahidic), he proposes that some of the development seen in the manuscript tradition is the result of a process of *Improvisationsschemata*, that is, of oral improvisations being recorded.[180] Budde's main focus is the different forms of **E-BAS**, and in many places he is able to highlight how Egyptian they are, particularly in the two Coptic recensions. Further, he suggests that what is shared between **E-BAS** and the Ω group is no more pronounced than the correspondences with other texts.[181] He gives particular attention to the relationship between **E-BAS** and **ByzBAS**, and finds no evidence for a particular relationship, suggesting they are no more than loose adaptions of a common tradition.[182] He does note parallels with the rest of the **BAS** family, but also with texts from across East and West Syria, Palestine and Egypt.[183] It is clear that this analysis questions the degree to which we can speak of an **Ur-BAS** in the sense that Engberding did, and clouds the relationship between **E-BAS** and Ω-**BAS** greatly.

Winkler's study focuses on the Syrian elements within the anaphora. Whilst largely accepting the general shape of Engberding's model, Winkler argues that **ArmBAS** preserves Ω-**BAS** better than any of the Ψ recensions.[184] This is largely based on the similarities of the use of

---

[180] McGowan, 'Basilian Anaphoras', 252. Note that Budde produces a comparative but not critical edition – his methodology requires he leave open the question of the 'original' form.

[181] He compares with **JAS** and *Nestorius*. Ibid., 255.

[182] Ibid.

[183] Ibid., 256.

[184] Winkler published her study as *Die Basilius-Anaphora: Edition Der Beiden Armenischen Redaktionem Und Der Relevanten Fragmente, Übersetzung Und Zusammenschau Aller Versionem Im Licht Der Orientalischen Überlieferungen*, Anaphorae Orientales 2, Anaphorae Armeniacae 2 (Pontifico Istituto Orientale, Rome, 2005). She has published English language summaries as 'The Christology of the Anaphora of Basil'; and 'On the Formation of the Armenian Anaphoras: A Completely Revised and Updated Overview' in *Studi Sull'Oriente Cristiano* 11, no. 2 (2007) 97–130. The latter work should not be confused with her 2001-2002 study, although it was not published until 2006, 'On the Formation of the Armenian Anaphoras: A Preliminary Overview' in Roberta R. Ervine (ed), *Worship Traditions in Armenia and the Neighboring Christian East: An International Symposium in Honor of the 40th Anniversary of St. Nersess Armenian Seminary*, Avant Series 3 (St. Vladimir's Seminary Press (with St. Nersess Armenian Seminary), Crestwood, 2006), 59–86. Winkler's work is also summarized by McGowan, 'Basilian Anaphoras', 238–46 with the critiques, 246-250. Given the importance of the Sanctus, and its surrounding texts, as an indicator in understanding the interconnections between the different anaphoras, a complete study should not

verbs in the doxological material in the preface, and at the institution narrative.[185] She also identifies a number of distinctively Syrian features which include: the ordering of the intercessions with prayer for the dead before the living;[186] the preference for scriptural Christological language, typical of the Antiochene synods of the fourth century, over the philosophical vocabulary of the Cappadocians;[187] language introducing the Sanctus reflecting Targum readings of Ezekiel and Isaiah regarding the angels;[188] and, of particular interest, the combination of the invitation for the Spirit to 'come' with the verb pair 'bless-sanctify' in the epiclesis which is found also in the East Syrian tradition.[189] The primary conclusion of Winkler's work relevant here is that the Syrian influence particularly apparent in the Armenian recensions suggests that it would be impossible to attribute **Ω-BAS** to Basil himself.

In light of the contributions of Budde and Winkler, we must be more reticent than Fenwick, to allow for the Syrian influence which Winkler finds and for the ambiguous relationship between **E-BAS** and **ByzBAS** resulting from their work; but we can, with some confidence, place the anaphora in the same milieu as Basil in one of its layers. Basil surely had influence in the development within the **Ω** group, certainly not the final redactor for every version in the group, and probably not starting with a text particularly close to **E-BAS**. Evidence, based on the work of Capelle and Bobrinskoy, identifies such influence in the Byzantine recension. This leaves open the question of why the name of Basil has been associated with the other variants. We must also acknowledge that the combined work of Winkler and Budde leaves the whole picture

---

omit Winkler's assessment of this issue in *Das Sanctus: Über Den Ursprung Und Die Anfänge Des Sanctus Und Sein Fortwirken*, Orientalia Christiana Analecta 267 (Pontificio Istituto Orientale, Rome, 2002).

[185] Winkler, 'The Christology of the Anaphora of Basil', 118–23.
[186] Winkler, 'Armenian Anaphoras', 112–13.
[187] That is to say that the language of οὐσία and ὁμοούσιος of the Cappadocians was not used. Winkler, 'The Christology of the Anaphora of Basil', 116–17.
[188] Winkler, 'Armenian Anaphoras', 127.
[189] Ibid., 116.

much less clear than it was for Engberding, and the first generations of scholars after him. Given the less-certain picture, Figure 1 may here be redrawn as shown in Figure 2, albeit with less confidence in it as a complete model than Engberding claimed.[190]

Figure 2: A Prospective Revised Model

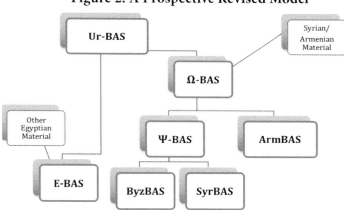

The Pneumatological Content of the Byzantine form of the Anaphora of Basil

The first material concerning the Holy Spirit in the anaphora is that found in the preface, an area covered by Capelle's study, who found close parallels in this section between **ByzBAS** and **DSS**, and Basil's other works, as evidence for Basil's editorial touch. He groups **ByzBAS**'s description of the Spirit in its preface into three parts, and whilst able to overlook the first as simply scriptural language, the others require

---

[190] As such, it is not obvious that **UrBAS** is best represented by **E-BAS**, and **Ω-BAS** may be best approximated by **ArmBAS**. Similarly, we must recognize that in its available form **E-BAS** may be later than **ByzBAS**. Further uncertainty must also apply to **SyrBAS**, which more properly belongs in association with **ArmBAS** than **ByzBAS**.

closer examination.[191] His groups are as follows:

	τὰς τῶν πατριαρχῶν εὐλογίας
3	τὴν ἐκ τῆς νομοθεσίας δεδομένην βοήθειαν
	τοὺς τύπους
1	τὰς προφητείας
	τὰ ἐν πολέμοις ἀνδραγαθήματα
2	τὰ διὰ τῶν δικαίων σημεῖα

In the second grouping, while the anaphora again follows a Pauline formula (Capelle cites 2 Cor. 1.22, 5.5 and Eph. 1.14 for the first phrase, Rom. 8.23 for the second, and Rom. 15.13 and 1 Cor. 15.45 for the third),[196] Capelle identifies similarities also to **DSS** 15,35[197] and 16,40[198] for the first phrase, to 15,36 for the second,[199] and 15,35 for the third.[200]He concludes that the similarities are not sufficiently precise to be conclusive.[201]

It is the third of these groups that Capelle finds most convincing. As well as a slight similarity to **Adv Eun**,[202] he finds very similar language and ideas expressed in **DSS** and Ep. 105. As given by Capelle:[203]

---

[191] He highlights John 16.13 and Rom. 8.15
[192] ET: 'the spirit of truth, the spirit of sonship' (after PEER, 117). Note that PE (p.232), along with LEW and Swainson, has this as υἱοθεσάς χάρισμα, (the grace of sonship) but that does not significantly affect Capelle's conclusion at this point, as the emphasis is on υἱοθεσάς as the descriptor of the Spirit acquired from Rom. 8.15.
[193] As above, here PE gives μελλούσης κληρονομίας, but the key focus is on the Sprit as ὁ ἀρραβών.
[194] ET: 'the pledge of the life to come, the first fruits of eternal good things, the life-giving power' (after PEER,117).
[195] ET: 'the fountain of sanctification, by whose enabling the whole rational and spiritual Creation does you service and renders you the unending doxology' (PEER, 117). As given by Capelle in *Témoin Archaïque*, 53.
[196] Capelle's text reads Rom. 18.13 (which does not exist), but the text he gives must be from 15.13.
[197] See at SC17 p. 368 ll. 43-44.
[198] SC17 p. 390 ll. 40-41.
[199] SC17 p. 370 ll. 10-11.
[200] SC17 p. 368 ll. 51-52.
[201] Doresse, Lanne, and Capelle, *Témoin Archaïque*, 53–54.
[202] Capelle points to the use of the phrase πηγὴ ἁγιασμοῦ in Adv Eun III.2. PG29 660C12.
[203] Doresse, Lanne, and Capelle, Témoin Archaïque, 55.

Anaphora[204]	ἡ πηγὴ τοῦ ἁγιασμοῦ, παρ' οὗ πᾶσα κτίσις λογική τε καὶ νοερὰ δυναμουμένη, σοὶ λατρεύει καὶ σοὶ τὴν ἀΐδιον ἀναπέμπει δοξολογίαν.
DSS 9,22[205]	ἁγιασμοῦ γένεσις, φῶς νοητόν, πάσῃ δυνάμει λογικῇ πρὸς τὴν τῆς ἀληθείας εὕρεσιν… παρεχόμενον.
DSS 16,38[206]	αἱ γὰρ καθαραὶ καὶ νοεραὶ καὶ ὑπερκόσμιοι δυνάμεις ἅγιαι καὶ εἰσὶ καὶ ὀνομάζονται, ἐκ τῆς παρὰ τοῦ ἁγίου Πνεύματος ἐνδοθείσης χάριτος τὸν ἁγιασμὸν κεκτημέναι.
DSS 16,38[207]	πῶς μὲν γὰρ εἴπωσιν ἄγγελοι Δόξα ἐν ὑψίστοις θεῷ μὴ δυναμωθέντες ὑπὸ τοῦ Πνεύματος;
Ep. 105[208]	Πνεῦμα ἅγιον, ἐκ θεοῦ τὴν ὕπαρξιν ἔχον, τὴν πηγὴν τῆς ἁγιότητος.

While there is no word-for-word correlation between any of these passages, a shared vocabulary and sense is apparent, or as Capelle puts it 'Aussi bien la formulation que la théologie, tout est pareil, sans qu'il y ait copie.' [209]

The Holy Spirit is mentioned in passing in relation to baptism in the relation of the salvific economy, where the description is that Christ 'sanctified [ἁγιάσας] us by the Holy Spirit'. This formulation and understanding is found in Basil, but is so wide-spread that no distinctive value can be attributed to it.

The next significant reference is the epiclesis. This is addressed to the Father, and reads:

We pray and beseech you, O holy of holies, in the good pleasure of

---

[204] I depart from Capelle here, who gives a Ω-BAS reconstruction; I quote **ByzBAS** as given by PE. The differences do not affect the comparison.

[205] ET: 'He is the source of holiness, an intellectual light for every rational power's discovery of truth, supplying clarity'. SC17 p. 324 ll. 26-29.

[206] ET: 'for the pure, intelligent, and other-worldly powers both are and are called holy because they have acquired holiness as a gift given to them by the Holy Spirit'. SC17 p. 376 ll. 3-5.

[207] ET: 'How could the angels say, "Glory to God in the highest", unless they have been empowered by the Holy Spirit?'. SC17 p. 382 ll. 61-62.

[208] ET: 'Holy Spirit, having his subsistence from God, Fount of holiness' (FC13 p. 230) PG32 513B1-2.

[209] Doresse, Lanne, and Capelle, *Témoin Archaïque*, 54–56

your bounty, that your [all-] Holy Spirit may come upon us and upon these gifts set forth, and bless them and sanctify and make this bread the precious body of our Lord and God and Saviour Jesus Christ. Amen. And this cup the precious blood of our Lord and God and Saviour Jesus Christ. Amen. Which is shed for the life of the world. Amen.

Unite with one another all of us who partake of the one bread and the

τὸ τῆς ἀληθείας πνεῦμα
τὸ τῆς υἱοθεσάς πνεῦμα [192]

ὁ ἀρραβὼν τῆς μελλούσης ζωῆς [195]
ἡ ἀπαρχὴ τῶν αἰωνίων ἀγαθῶν
ἡ ζωοποιὸς δύναμις [194]

ἡ πηγὴ τοῦ ἁγιασμοῦ, παρ᾽ οὗ πᾶσα κτίσις λογικὴ τε καὶ νοερὰ
δυναμουμένη, σοὶ λατρεύει καὶ σοὶ τὴν ἀίδιον ἀναπέμπει
δοξολογίαν.[195]

cup into fellowship with the one Holy Spirit; and make none of us to partake of the holy body and blood of your Christ for judgement…

σοῦ δεόμεθα καὶ σὲ παρακαλοῦμεν ἅγιε ἁγίων εὐδοκίᾳ τῆς σῆς ἀγαθότητος ἐλθεῖν τὸ Πνεῦμά σου τὸ πανάγιον ἐφ᾽ ὑμᾶς καὶ ἐπὶ τὰ προκείμενα δῶρα ταῦτα καὶ εὐλογῆσαι αὐτὰ καὶ ἁγιάσαι καὶ ἀναδεῖξαι. Τὸν μὲν ἄρτον τοῦτον αὐτὸ τὸ τίμιον σῶμα τοῦ κυρίου καὶ θεοῦ καὶ σωτῆρος ἡμῶν Ἰησοῦ Χριστοῦ. ἀμήν. Τὸ δὲ ποτήροιν τοῦτο αὐτὸ τὸ τίμιον αἷμα τοῦ κυρίου καὶ θεοῦ καὶ σωτῆρος ἡμῶν Ἰησοῦ Χριστοῦ. ἀμήν. τὸ ἐκχυθὲν ὑπὲρ τῆς τοῦ κόσμου ζωῆς. ἀμήν.

Ἡμᾶς δὲ πάντας τοὺς ἐκ τοῦ ἑνὸς ἄρτου καὶ τοῦ ποτηρίου μετέχοντας ἑνῶσαι ἀλλήλοις εἰς ἑνὸς Πνεύματος ἁγίου κοινωνίαν καὶ μηδένα ἡμῶν εἰς κρίμα…

Whatever we think was the precise original relationship between this prayer and **E-BAS**, it is clear that the theology of the epiclesis is more developed. **E-BAS** has a simple invocation over the elements and over the people, for the consecration of the elements to be 'holy of holies' and for the worthy reception by the communicants.[210] Both elements are also present in this revised form, and whilst some of the same language is retained, its use is different. In particular, we see here greater precision in describing the transformation of the elements.[211]

It is clear from **DSS** 27,66 that Basil attached significance to the epiclesis. He defends it as a necessary addition to scriptural forms, alongside a turning to the East for prayer and the signing with the cross.[212]While we do not get a statement as explicit on the role of the Spirit as some of John Chrysostom's statements – '[the bread] through the Spirit descending on it is made Heavenly Bread'[213] – it is clear that Basil finds this a necessary liturgical action. It is therefore no surprise to find a developed text in an anaphora under his hand.

While, following Winkler, identifying the verb pair 'bless-sanctify' as a typical Syrian usage, the third verb, rendered into English as 'make', ἀναδεῖξαι, is also used by Basil in **DSS**. Basil has 'ἐπὶ τῇ ἀναδείξει τοῦ ἄρτου τῆς εὐχαριστίας…', that is 'at the making of the bread of the Eucharist…'.[214] This suggests it is conceivable that to the older form (bless-sanctify), ἀναδεῖξαι is added to pick up on a Basilian understanding of the consecration of the elements, as the text of the epiclesis is expanded

---

[210] The epiclesis of **E-BAS** reads '[We] pray you…your Holy Spirit may descend upon us and upon these gifts that have been set before you, and may sanctify them and make them holy of holies. Make us all worthy to partake of your holy things for sanctification of soul and body, that we may become one body and one spirit, and may have a portion with all the saints…'. ET: PEER,71.

[211] Bobrinskoy, 'Liturgie et Ecclésiologie', 9–10.

[212] The latter presumably at baptism.

[213] John Chrysostom *In Joannem*: Hom. 45,2. ET: NPNF1-14 p. 161. Equally, however, in Chrysostom we cannot overlook statements that appear to grant the consecration to the Institution Narrative – see, for example, *De proditione Judae* 1,2.

[214] **DSS** 27,66.

to be more explicitly consecratory.

The later part of the epiclesis is more significant. Bobrinskoy highlights, in comparison with **CHR** and many other anaphoras, how communion with the Spirit is here the 'mode fondamental' of participation rather than just one of several fruits of reception.[215] Communion, κοινωνία, of the Spirit is a central theme for Basil's pneumatology. It is central to his understanding of the internal relationships of the Trinity, and also to human participation in the Godhead.

Basil uses κοινωνία to speak of the relationship between the Father and the Son,[216] of the Spirit's relationship with the Father and the Son,[217] of the shared nature of the Spirit and God.[218] For Basil, that the Spirit is in κοινωνία with the Father and the Son is a statement of the Spirit's divinity. It is also in such a communion with the Spirit that Basil presents human salvation, whether this is presented in the sense of separation from the Spirit as a cutting off,[219] or the more positive statement that 'The Spirit illuminates those who have been cleansed from every stain and makes them spiritual by means of communion with himself.'[220] Basil is also clear that is a corporate activity, binding one to another, not individualistic.[221]

While none of this explicitly restates the request of the epiclesis, it shows that what is asked for in the anaphora summarizes an essential point of Basil's pneumatology, that communion with one another in the Spirit is central to the salvific economy.

Two final references are made to the Spirit, the first at the end of the intercessions and then again in the final doxology:

...quickly destroy the uprising of heresies by the power of your Holy

---

[215] Bobrinskoy, 'Liturgie et Ecclésiologie', 16.
[216] **DSS** 6,15
[217] **DSS** 19,48
[218] **DSS** 13,30. Bobrinskoy gives some further uses also, 'Liturgie et Ecclésiologie', 19.
[219] **DSS** 16,40.
[220] **DSS** 9,23. Again more examples of Basil's use may be found in Bobrinskoy, 'Liturgie et Ecclésiologie', 20–21.
[221] See **DSS** 26,61.

Spirit… and grant us with one mouth and one heart to glorify and hymn your all-honourable and magnificent name, the Father and the Son and the Holy Spirit, now [and always and to the ages of ages.]

…τὰς τῶν αἱρέσεων ἐπαναστάσεις ταχέως κατάλυσον ἐν τῇ δυνάμει τοῦ ἁγίου σου πνεύματος… Καὶ δὸς ἡμῖν ἐν ἑνὶ στόματι καὶ μιᾷ καρδίᾳ δοξάζειν καὶ ἀνυμνεῖν τὸ πάντιμον καὶ μεγαλοπρεπὲς ὄνομά σου τοῦ Πατρὸς καὶ τοῦ Υἱοῦ καὶ ἁγίου Πνεύματος νῦν [καὶ ἀεὶ καὶ εἰς τοὺς αἰῶνας τῶν αἰώνων.]

In most contexts the doxology says little about the pneumatology of the text, but, given the prominent place doxological forms take in **DSS**, it cannot be ignored here, not least because, given the case Basil has made in the treatise, this is in the 'wrong' form. Basil, while accepting the orthodoxy of the uncoordinated form of doxology found here, is seeking to promote the use of a coordinated form – that is to say, he is arguing for a formula akin to 'the Father with the Son in the Spirit'.

It is interesting here to compare **ByzBAS** with the other recensions. In **SyrBAS**, whilst it is expanded in form, the doxology is addressed to the Father, 'along with' the Son 'and' the Spirit. **ArmBAS** reflects the same form with regard to the Son but favours 'with' for the Spirit. **E-BAS** has 'through Jesus Christ and the Holy Spirit' but adds what appears to be a deliberate statement of the unity of the Godhead.[222]

Prior to Winkler's work, this could be understood as supporting the idea that Basil was involved in the recension of **Ω-BAS** or with the Syrian and Armenian recensions.[223] While it is impossible to rule out such influence categorically, Winkler's work suggests that the coordinated form was earlier, and has been eliminated from **ByzBAS**. In that case, we must either attribute it to another hand, or a conciliatory effort on

---

[222] See Fenwick, *Basil and James*, 286–87.
[223] The conclusions of Fenwick in this regard are interesting; see ibid., 299–301.

Basil's part, attempting to avoid unnecessary conflict – conflict against which Basil does argue firmly, positing that 'silence [is] more useful than speech'. Providing the result is not 'blaspheming the Spirit', we might expect Basil to be accepting of it.[224]

The reference to the power of the Spirit destroying heresies is interesting. Clearly Basil lived in a world where the threat and challenge of heresy was real and public – and it was quite common for a bishop to be deposed as a heretic only to be restored later.[225]While expecting the question of heresy to be of import in the life of prayer, it is, however, not apparent which heresy the redactor had in mind.

In this context, we can say that the idea of the Spirit being the person of the Godhead that would act in this way is coherent with Basil's picture of the Spirit. Nevertheless, it is hard to tie it to Basil in any particular sense. That the Spirit is one who acts against heresy fits with his model of the economic Trinity but is never given as an explicit example.

Conclusion

There are far fewer signs of connection apparent in the texts considered in this chapter than seen in the previous chapter. In part, this is because there is a greater sense – because we can see more of the layers of the development – of **BAS** as 'living literature' than was visible with the *Sacramentary of Sarapion*.[226]As a result, there is no clear and direct link between Basil's doctrinal material and the anaphora.

Despite this, we are still able to draw a number of connections that show an interaction between the doctrinal work of the Cappadocians and the liturgical environs. It is first and foremost obvious that liturgical action and formula underpin the doctrine developed by Basil in particular. His use of the formula of baptism is not just a discussion of

---

[224] **DSS** 30,76-79.
[225] We considered Athanasius previously, but we could also note the way Basil is involved in the opposition to Eustathius and Eunomius.
[226] cf. Paul F. Bradshaw, 'Liturgy and "Living Literature"' in Paul F. Bradshaw and Bryan Spinks (edd), *Liturgy in Dialogue* (SPCK, London, 1993) 138–53.

the scriptural text of Matthew 28.19, but is rooted in practice, and is central to his argument for the divinity of the Spirit.

We can see a connection between Basil's understanding of the epistemic role of the Spirit and the necessity of the action of the Spirit expressed in the epiclesis to 'bless… sanctify… and make' the elements into the body and blood of Christ. It is clear that for Basil, there is an identity between the ability of the Spirit to reveal God and the Spirit's own divinity. So, if God is revealed in an action, then this must be through the Spirit. Thus, we can conclude that in Basil's thinking, the activity of the Spirit is essential to the consecration of the elements – in the sense of the epiclesis, only the Spirit 'makes'.

In the same way, and whilst recognizing the Syrian link, Winkler has identified in the origin of the verb-pair, we can see how the verb 'sanctify' fits perfectly in a Basilian epiclesis. Just as the Spirit has the epistemic role of making the Son known – either in general or in the eucharistic elements – the Spirit also is the one sanctifying. Again, for Basil, this is both necessary and sufficient to the Spirit's divinity – only the divine can divinise.

Another major theme of Basil's pneumatology is the sense of the Spirit as the Spirit of knowledge. While there is only a tenuous link, such a sense might suggest that the Spirit is the one who defends against heresy, as in the final part of the anaphora. While not contrary to Basil's pneumatology, this may be an argument from silence. Finally, in regard to the anaphoral doxology, we have a formula that is acceptable and orthodox to Basil, though not the form which we would expect him to have chosen himself.

We are left with significant difficulty in establishing any systematic linking between the liturgical text and Basil's doctrinal work. The work of Bobrinskoy and Capelle has shown that there are some literary similarities in some parts of the text, so that we can remain open to the possibility of Basil's involvement in the development of the anaphora – nonetheless we must remain open to the possibility that much of this stems from the *Formelgut* from which it was composed. However, Winkler, in particular, has clearly demonstrated that there is sufficient complexity in the development of the anaphoral tradition commonly named for Basil that it would be difficult to isolate his contributions, and thereby to see confidently how his theology is displayed liturgically.

4

Conclusions

These two case studies require us to draw different conclusions. My consideration of the *Sacramentary of Sarapion* alongside the theological writings of Athanasius has shown some clear links in the pneumatological language and approach used. In considering **BAS**, however, no such clear particular conclusions are possible with regard to its connections to its theological environment.

Within **BAS**, there are certainly signs of links to the language Basil used in his treatise **DSS**. Nevertheless, as Winkler and Budde have independently demonstrated, there are many strata to the development of the anaphora as it has been preserved, with Syrian and Egyptian influences seemingly present. This does not amount to evidence that there is no influence of contemporary theological developments on liturgical prayer. Indeed, the trace influences of Basil's writings indicate that this link may have existed. Nevertheless, the chain and the development of these theological links is not sufficiently clear within the liturgical text to draw confident conclusions. Chiefly, this uncertainty must be attributed to the development of the anaphora, which has not preserved its sources. That is to say, the same uncertainty that must be applied to the reconstruction of the anaphora's history, also must apply to the theological sources upon which it drew.

In contrast, because the *Sacramentary* has been preserved from an earlier form than the Basiline texts, and although the extant manuscript is later, it more closely reflects the earlier generation of source material. In the case of this text, it seems clear that the theological environment from which this text stems is that shaped by Athanasius and the early pneumatology which his thought represents. We cannot remove all uncertainty though: we simply do not have enough data to conclude whether the theological statements prompted the liturgical development or *vice versa*. Nevertheless, commonality of language and style used to talk of the Spirit in particular, and of the Trinity more generally, necessitates the conclusion that the two must have developed in the same milieu.